The Girl and the Pig

An Epic Tale

by T. L. Jones

DORRANCE
PUBLISHING CO
EST. 1920
PITTSBURGH, PENNSYLVANIA 15222

The contents of this work, including, but not limited to, the accuracy of events, people, and places depicted; opinions expressed; permission to use previously published materials included; and any advice given or actions advocated are solely the responsibility of the author, who assumes all liability for said work and indemnifies the publisher against any claims stemming from publication of the work.

Dorrance Publishing Co., Inc.
701 Smithfield Street
Pittsburgh, PA 15222
Visit our website at *www.dorrancebookstore.com*

ISBN: 978-1-4809-0886-4
eISBN: 978-1-4809-0748-5

Thank You

To my two sons: Charles and Patrick. No matter how crazy I seem or how much I feel I fail, they never treated me with contempt. They have treated me only with support, respect, and love. Also, to the people who told me, "You know, you should write a book." So, I guess the real thank you goes to the Person behind each one of those people: the Holy Spirit of God. To each person who took their turn, unbeknownst to each other:

Dr. Mark Means
Rusty Jacksland
Patrick Smith
Charles Smith
Johnny Mims
Tina Pettit
and
Patrick Ross

I dedicate this book to:

Trauma Survivors

They are survivors.

If you don't have respect for their strength, you can't be of any help. It is a privilege that they let you in—there is no reason they should trust you—NONE. You can't know their terror. It is your worst nightmare come true; a nightmare from which you never awaken. It is unrelenting. There has been no safety; no one, no time, no place, no thing—all was tainted. Hope was obliterated time and time again. That they would go to anyone for help is a supreme act of valor.

With All My Respect:

Author Unknown

Preface

Very rarely, if ever, does anyone who experiences the challenges I have faced from childhood become anything that appears planned. When everything you've got is utilized to stay alive, the question of what you want to be when you grow up is a luxury never reasonably explored and is usually lost within the quest of simply trying to figure out who you are. Looking back, there is one thing for certain that has been in my heart to do since whenever—to write.

The story *behind* this story is very cool *and* supernatural. This is one of those books that, as I reread, I am filled with a sense of awe that I even wrote it. One morning, at about 2:00 or 3:00 AM, I woke up rather suddenly, as if someone had given me a stern elbow to the ribs. I sat up hearing lines of poetry going through my head as if someone was reading them to me. (I blame the Holy Spirit for that.) My first instincts to disregard what I was hearing quickly dissolved into an urgency to write it down, for I actually began to pay attention to the words themselves. It was a story about a little girl raised on the farm by a pig. By the time I found pen and paper, I was already listening to line 7 or 8, and all I could do was hope I could remember the start, catch up to where I was, and not disrupt this amazing flow. This had never happened before. As I was quickly writing what I heard, it took me until about page 3 to realize that this story was about me. It was overwhelming. Since Papa (my awesome Heavenly Father) had never worked with me this way before, it also made this particular event even more difficult to comprehend. For once, I left off trying to figure it out so I wouldn't miss anything. It is difficult to write while you cry. That was the first poem. Over the course of the next couple of years, this event was repeated. I also simply began writing on my own, covering everything I had to deal with to become a whole person. It was a therapy I actually enjoyed. Each poem stood alone. Several notebooks became full and eventually lay in a pile, collecting dust until the day Papa began to pester me about writing a book. Although it was in my heart to do, I belittled the idea. Isn't the world already riddled with tragic stories and personal/spiritual victories? One of the many things I am thankful for is that once Papa *starts on you* about something, He will not let it go, and it always turns out beautiful. As I am prone to do (with much less gusto now), I argued with Papa that I had nothing to write about. To prove the point I had nothing to offer, I grabbed my laptop, pulled up a blank page, and sat there, waiting for something to *hit* me. It did not. Figuring I had proven my point, I closed the lid and put it out of my mind.

Several days later, I found the pile of notebooks where my individual poems had been gathering dust. I began to revisit them from the very beginning, being impressed I had actually kept them intact for that long. When I write, I am so critical of myself that it all ends up in the garbage. What hit me took me to my knees. Papa opened my eyes to the fact that every single one of these poems *went together* and was already in a chronologically correct state. Remove the titles, write more lines for connectivity, and voila!—my book was already written. The amount of poetry needed for connectivity turned out to be vast with very few of the originals ending up like they began (better, actually). But I came alive with the idea, and the fiery passion to see it through was innate.

The subject matter is disturbing—I admit. Most people cannot bear to think of it, and, for that reason, aside from counselor's visits, me and people like me are shamed to silence. Yes, even still today. I also used that reason to keep my book sitting mostly unfinished; like the notebooks, it was gathering dust. I wasn't convinced I was capable enough to tell any valuable story, for I was still wearing, on the inside, the tattered clothes of my abuses and what they had done to me. Not only is the subject matter disturbing, but I also have an unashamed attachment to my God and His Love. I don't care if you agree with me on my spiritual beliefs. My hope is that you will find what you need to stand a little bit taller and a little bit straighter with a little bit (or a lot) more hope after your visit.

From 2008 to 2012, before this book was written, I was privileged to serve the town I live in as a law enforcement officer (LEO). I *loved* my job. I got to make things right for people. I learned a lot, and the sad fact is this: not only am I not alone in this *epic tale* that begins tragically, but also the sheer numbers of those who can personally relate to this is *staggering*. Every call to which I was dispatched was loaded with people I could completely relate to. It was my privilege to dispel the myth 911 callers had that I (this *got-it-together-looking person*) knew nothing about their broken down, beaten up lives. If anything, it was my honor to be a testimony to the fact that with Papa, there *is* life and hope after abuse—*no matter how severe*. I took the PTSD (posttraumatic stress disorder) test. The results? I should be dead. No joke. In the experience of those who made this test, there was simply no need to score beyond a 9—you should be dead after that anyway. My score was well past 10.

Abuse (including manipulation and hypocrisy) in all its forms is passed down from generation to generation. I decided, when I was eighteen, that no stone would be left unturned and nothing left to chance. I would throw everything I knew and everything I had been taught away, so that by *faith* with Papa alone, I could build transparency and truth in both my life and the lives of my children. Papa looked down at my generation and chose me to change the tide. He knew I would not waste my turn in carrying the torch. This work—what it took to survive it, face it, and change it—is dedicated to my boys. Having no blueprint to raise them and not liking what I saw in others either, I have done well—never perfect but definitely an original and always forgiven.

To My Boys

Whatever, in raising you, I have missed
My desire to change is my final kiss.
As you leave my home to live your life
With your courage to change you'll be all right.
Papa will care for and honor you
As you walk with Him and keep plowing through.
My biggest passion has always been
To set you up so you can win.
With Papa I've fought and changed the tide,
Our family curses, with me, have died.
But again, whatever I have missed
My life of change is my final kiss.

The Girl and The Pig:
An Epic Tale

There once was a little girl raised by a pig
Who taught his whole family to snort and to dig.
He taught her to wallow in fear and to stink
But never, no never allowed her to think.
He beat her to teach her the trades of "give more."
Some of her names were "Bitch," "Slut," and "Whore."
She never believed she'd been made from above,
Although she had been told many stories of love.
Her instructor for life was a cowardly swine,
His lessons were simple and singular: "MINE."

Her abusive hell was starkly contrasted
With lessons from church; from the pulpit was blasted
The "pearls of truth" from a handwritten letter—
Apparently if she prayed it's supposed to get better.
As Slut would go to try on the Pearls
Pig would insist, "Only For PROPER girls!
Your job is to wallow, you whore, and to stink
And never, no never is your job to think!"
So along with her mother, Slut prayed and Slut sang
But God didn't work—it all stayed the same.
As pigs often do and as pigs often are

Being far too pigheaded to cease from his mire
Not once did Pig take the time to realize
Slut HAD to think if she were to survive.
She got awfully good and was quick as could be;
They had no idea she was A.D.D.

A bad family curse needs a great family gift.
Multitasking to live was constant and quick.
She worked and perfected the art of the tacit
Implied rules of chaos and every known facet
Of everything everyone believed she should be:
Intelligent, mutilated, fun and carefree.
Pig, and in ways that were constant and brutal,
Insisted that females were useless and futile.
Pig said, "LOGIC is what you must seek.
Emotions in females are what makes them weak."
She took Pig's advice and gave up the notion
Of normal assimilation of human emotion.
Feeling at all, she believed, was insane,
So she denied herself and became inhumane.

One of Whore's great many steps toward disaster
Was copying Pig, her abuser and master.
Her misapplied efforts of proficiency
Made her far more logical than he'd ever be.
"I'll show you," cried her battered heart
"I'll gain your acceptance doing MORE than my part."
She refused to believe that Pig didn't care
After all Pig's her father, he just wouldn't dare.
"I'll simply work harder and one day he'll see
All the potential inside of me."

Outside the house on any bright day
Slut could be found with her friends out to play.
Baby dolls, trees, spiders or ball
No matter the past time she mastered them all.

A determined girl and very aware,
Answering quickly to a "double-dog-dare,"
Going and doing what others would not
Just by being told, that she could not.
The smallest player in football games
Meant the "law of gross tonnage" would force her to change
To different tactics to ensure their defeat—
No matter their size, they can't run without feet!

With music and school she was labeled as "gifted,"
An overachiever that never drifted
Into the ways she was told, "She ought not."
So mindful was Whore, of what she was taught
That what's most important is what others see—
Make it look as perfect as you wish it would be.
She held her head high as she "towed the line";
Hypocritical truths turn very dark over time.

Lives that are crafted through manipulation
Have cinder block walls for segregation.
Holding opposing values alike
Is a requirement for a broken life.
To resist true change but stay on your feet
Is to make sure opposing views never meet.

We fast-forward this tale that will brutally be
Complicated by something called "puberty."
After all this is when a child in their season,
Begins their task of independent reason.
With insight and brilliance they compare and apply
What they've been taught with the question of "why."
The conclusions they draw will compel them to do
Or not, whatever you told them to.
The battle that's waged, what you often see,
Is brought on by parental hypocrisy.
You taught with your lips to question and prove

But you get mad when it's turned upon you.
The parental response of "because I said so"
Is no longer good enough and you blow
Up and position yourself for the win...
Now it's about controlling them.
Analytical children will see and will catch
All the ways your insides and outsides don't match.
I firmly believe that this is God's way
Of exposing the truth of law vs. Grace.
Law demands there must be control
While Love through Grace transforms the soul.
The parent's goal should not be to win
But accepting their own transformation within.
The tumultuous anger that begins to dwell
Under the roof you used to know well
Is shrugged off with each excuse that you give
As they ignore what you say and DO what you've lived.

This too, happened to poor ugly Slut,
As her A.D.D caused her to quickly wake up.
The inconsistencies she found to be vast
She'd been set up to fail no matter the task.
Her life of acceptance she had hoped to pursue
Turned into one great big "catch-22."
Her complications had gotten far worse
As the destruction of her family curse
Began to unfold and provoke her to anger—
Welcome to High School, the life of a teenager.
She helplessly watched as what she'd been taught
Would not help her now, oh no, it would not.
The logic and law she had used to survive
Became an implosion as Love was denied.
Confusing emotions, once kept at bay,
Became stubbornly nosey and would not go away.
They refused to stay buried and she'd had enough
Which caused her, without warning, to occasionally blow up.

God showed mercy and gave her the chance
To breathe, she poured herself into dance.
She became the mascot of her school.
Anonymity's reward? Being cool.
All year long she got to do
Exactly what she wanted to.
Pep rallies and games people laughed and cheered,
She was finally accepted; people finally cared.
All year long, in turn, they begged to know
Who it was that put on such a wonderful show.
But she held on and would not tell;
Her actions would prove they would all do well
To accept the person behind the mask;
Surely this was not an impossible task!

The moment of truth finally came
At the last pep rally, the Homecoming game.
The bleachers soon emptied as they rushed the floor
To carry their mascot, with cheers, out the door.
Now is the time! She bravely believed,
That her acceptance had been finally achieved.
Out of the silence, she heard a gasp
As she began taking off her mask.
What began as an excited hush
Turned into a silence of bitter disgust.
It took many years to get over the fact
That they all simply frowned and turned their backs.
For the rest of the year she endured the glares
That simply reinforced that nobody cared.

The darkness that follows this laborious mess
Can only be described as demonic, at best.

In Slut's epic quest, now comes the part
That is no longer for the faint of heart.
If you'd like, you can simply skip to the end

Where God is the Victor and He gets the win.
But when you can manage, be it later or now,
Read all of the GOOD in the details of how
The story that Satan should surely have won
Gets overwritten by Love through God's Son.

It is time:

No longer narrator, I make my confession
And switch "she" to "I" and take full possession.
This story is mine, the struggles specific.
My biggest complaint: to go back and revisit.
But God through direction, desire and advice
Suggested I write this far more than twice.
As obedient I've been, obedient I'll stay
And trust God will use this in whatever way
That His plan was and always has been...
Enough with the chitchat; let us begin.

I remember the day at the young age of four,
Born in '70 so must've been '74.
I saw something that is usually discreet,
A sexual predator across my street.
Practicing his trade and looking at me
I had no clue of what should or shouldn't be.
My mom finding out what had kept my attention
Quickly removed me and gave it a mention
To Pig, whom you think would put this to ends,
But Pig being pig, quickly made friends.

With no recollection of how, where or when
My memories just stop and pick up again.
Five years later in '79,
Far as I knew I was doing just fine.
But as I would listen to other kids talk
About their memories in their memory walk
I became more uncomfortably aware
Those five years of my life simply weren't there.

In my time line of life are great empty spaces
Where Polaroid's hang that take the place of
A life that's hauntingly just disappeared;
I never asked why, it was bizarre and weird.
The pictures I have in that space are disturbing,
And reek of a five-year-old's new understanding
Of life and what her purpose must be;
Sponsored by Pig and his friend 'cross the street.

My mother gave Pig only one flaw
And that was his love of alcohol.
Finding out, years later, how much she knew
I screamed with rage, "Where were you?"
I also to God, did pose and insist
This question of mine went something like this:

Shared in rape, imprisoned, confused—
I have just one question: Where were you?

Mistreated, hated, beaten, accused—
I have just one question: Where were you?

I was trying to survive an explosive gale
While praying for death to finally exhale.
I've tried to end it while no one knew.
If you cared so much, where were you?

I carved my flesh, my pain being real,
With my trusted friend of Damascus steel.
"It's what you deserve!" my soul cried, too,
And my only question: Where were you?

Watching a girl get torn apart
Who tried to please with all her heart;
She believed she did what she's 'sposed to do;
My question remains: Where were you?

Did you sit there enjoying the perversion and grief?
Like the temperamental gods of the Greeks?
Did you ever take notice, even a few?
Then answer this question: Where were you?

You said that you loved me day after day
While you sang, you churched, you praised, you prayed;
With fear as your master you let NOTHING through—
IT WAS YOUR JOB! So, where were you?

With your head in the clouds and your face to the sky
Singing hymns of the sweet by and by
I have lost my respect for your god and for you.
IT WAS YOUR JOB! Where were you?

"Remember your God as He splits the Red Sea"
Then how, oh Lord, did you remember me?
I know that you WATCHED, but what did you DO?
Which is why I ask—Where were you?

I am angry and hurt 'cause you're not here to stay.
Your love was just lip service day after day.
I wish that you loved me like you say that you do.
My question is fair: Where were you?

My heart makes a grimace; I can't help but wince,
I now know my God so much better than this.
But humans are humans in horrible times
And God's not the author of any such crimes.
As you read and tell others please take this to heart
God showed me, much later, His glorious part.
The mercy He showed me while under attack
Broke through while reading a book called *The Shack*.

God could have easily left me with all
Of every detail to recall.
But instead His Spirit wrapped 'round my head
And kept me from all those details of dread.
Now, the only things that are left behind
Are the scars that only "those that know" find.

It's amazingly awesome in an int'resting way
That no matter how dif'rent we each wish to stay
The same evil leaves an identical mess.
Makes finding the broken easier, I guess.

I've seen drunken rages; I've been called a whore;
I've been thrown onto pianos and more.
I've seen my mom bleed; we've run for our lives;
I watched Pig try and commit suicide...

The suicide season—now let's stop right here.
This is when God made it perfectly clear
That if I did not take Him as my Lord and Master
My life was doomed to a Xeroxed disaster.
I remember that moment with such clarity.
Like *A Christmas Carol*, my God let me see
My future without Him; I shook to my core.
"I accept your forgiveness, please show me no more!"
God moved inside, I got a short stop
As I basked with peace on the Mountaintop
Where each of us gets to be for a bit
As we first commune with the Holy Spirit.

I was set free; Pig got a pass on his guilt
And we continued on in the same mess he'd built.
His hugs were too long; his hands liked to wander
And mom blamed me for his drunken blunder.
Rejected at home, rejected at school.
I lived my life by rejection's rule.
God said that He loved me or so it would seem—
But what did the word "love" even mean?
Nothing at all to a life truly stuck
In the foundations of "I don't measure up."

Taking Pig's lead it was always implied
That the family would be better off if I died,
For I am the reason our family's so broken;
These were the words that were tacitly spoken.

Hypocrisy's deadliest quality
Is found in its deniability.
It is never spoken, only implied
And for that reason it can be denied.
When what you say and what you do
Is congruent to only one person, YOU,
The gap you deny provokes those in your charge

To a resentment that will grow very large.
So, when what you end up with is not what you meant,
Hypocrisy is usually the cul-per'rit.
Stealthy hypocrisies lay far below
Between the "us" that we are and the "us" that we show.
To see it takes courage, transparency and trust
And walking by Faith—a misunderstood must.
To ask for truth once is never enough!
Denial is a mind-set that proves to be tough.
You must take a year or better yet more
And let God tear down and not let you ignore
The truth of some things while you let others go.
The denials you keep, like kudzu, will grow.

Let's park on this subject for a while at least
For the damage of hypocrisy is Satan's feast.
I've listened closely to kids of all kinds,
Whether Pastor's or Deacon's or Elder's to find
They despise the control and can't wait to bolt.
This should give us all a "waking up" jolt.
Seeing this trend gave my heart a new goal,
To find out what it was that corroded their soul.
My question to God was: "What can it be
That causes these children to want to be free?
If we have the Truth and we're doing it right
What I'm seeing is hopeless and gives me a fright!
Don't take this wrong; I'm determined as ever;
I'm begging You now to help me do better.
I'm no Christian "giant"; it must be complex
If even the Pastor's cannot do what's best!
I'm going to beg you and not let it go.
I'm terribly broken so I NEED to know,
Will everything I do truly not matter
And I'll have no choice but to watch my kids shatter
Their relationship with You and with me?
No matter what—they'll long to be free?"

People like me from a background so broken
Have to accept the obvious notion,
Our blueprint is bad; there is nothing worth lasting
On with the next generation that's passing.
I suggest there is more than just little proof
That all should do what I've done with the truth.
Challenge your blueprint and throw all away
And with Love by Faith, build what should stay.
Your blueprint, no matter the prayer or the thought
That was placed with each brick will have cracks throughout.
The Doc's never called for the well, but the sick.
If you think you're "okay" then you'll never get fixed.
What God's longing heart wishes for us to see
Is no matter our past we are all sickly!
I have laid my foundations of law with care,
Backed up with scripture and there's cracks everywhere!
Our first encounter? Teenager rebellion.
For with their behavior they are actually tellin'
Anyone that will listen as best they know how
That they see all of your inconsistencies now.
For next generations to keep up the pace,
Requires the Master apply much Grace!

Transparency, Love and trusting His promise
Of His wonderful work will bring peace upon us.
Please learn something of "Cause and Effect"
Because what we DO is what they reflect.
When what you teach and what you live
Doesn't match up, something will give.
Your children will definitely let you know
By the measure of respect they simply can't show.
For it is a rule God set forth long ago,
The only things Children are able to show
Are where they have come from and what they have seen.
They are your mirror, so what this means
Is by the time that their questions are made

Their foundations, by you, have been solidly laid.

I have, many times, hated to see
Hypocritical foundations crafted by me.
I knew I had placed it and Wisdom showed how
I put the crack in that wall that shows now.
A brick I had laid through actions sincere,
Turned very ugly year after year.
My face hit the floor to beg God how
To fix hypocrisies in their life, somehow.
I acknowledge I did it, I also know why,
But I can't fix it—please hear my cry!
Praise God for His mercy, for I could not see,
For Him to fix them, He started with me!
As He fixed my bricks, I could fix theirs.
I needed much wisdom to climb those stairs.
I firmly believed it was all on me—
To ensure my perfection so my children would be
So much more obliged to submit to my lead.
My parental summons calls; I will succeed.

"It is time to study! To church I will go!"
Absolutes make it hard to say, "I don't know."
It builds our pride and crushes our soul,
Studying so much brings God under control.
Can you know Him completely? You have such gall!
To understand God will make Him too small!
As knowledge becomes your "golden calf"
God longs to show you, "You don't know the half!"

An idol we make through absolutes,
As we study to show ourselves approved.
We constantly strive to be in control,
And because it is scripture we rename the goal.
We replace trusting God as we trust in our study.
The outside's "spot on" but the insides are muddy.

If I studied enough I just knew I would find
Golden nuggets of truth that would be all mine.
I wanted to please! Be an overachiever!
"God's cream of the crop!" A "top-notch believer!"
What God calls "judging," I call "shoot."
The damage is equal, the aftermath is moot.
After salvation I studied and worked
To earn my acceptance; I became quite a jerk.
I could quote scripture and do what was told
While my life on the outside, reeked of control.
The more vast my knowledge, the stiffer my neck,
As I won my debates with apologetics.

The lessons I learned? Anything but bliss;
As I recall, it went something like this:

Black and white, right and wrong
If you don't know the difference then you don't belong.
Black and white, right and wrong
Hold the rifle to your shoulder and be strong.
Don't worry, my child, you do them a favor.
Righteousness comes in only one flavor.
Shoot often and shoot with skill.
Do not understand them; shoot to kill.
This home church is the perfect place
To become strong in toxic faith.
To work and claim some righteous station
In judgmental indignation.
I get to play with warped little blocks
While I keep God in a warped little box.
I search the scriptures to "see if it's so"
To decide who can stay and who should go.
As I listen I am using the slant
Of, since I have studied, I know God can't.
My job is to study every jot and tittle;
Using it to shoot you for standing in the middle.

With knowledge we shall judge them,
"It is for the best, my dear"
After all, it is written, "He is love" and "God is near."
So take a toxic faith, learn it well and teach in kind,
And as our churches empty, God may ask us to prove and find,
Any place within the scriptures—any place in which we knew
Where God or Christ Himself said we could Love and shoot
them, too.

It's not about being the Biblical Scholar,
It's all about Love and removing law's collar!
Our massive failure has turned out be
The truth we find in transparency.
Just like salvation, simple yet hard
And carries a payback no one can afford.
It is quite sad; I'd simply changed my abuser,
From Pig to church and the laws of their scripture.

Now, where was I? Oh, yes! I had just gotten saved!
And what do you know? My home never changed!
Turmoil and rage; I became labeled;
Adding God to my chaos reduced Him to fables.
All I could do was survive and demand.
But even survival required God's hand.

Several dark times, a total of three;
I decided to take my own life to be free.
Once, at fifteen, I tried to end
My life with some pills I had bought from a "friend."
Each failed attempt would end with great fear,
For God made His sovereignty miraculously clear.
But soon I'd forget as I drowned in the mess
And would try once again to end my hopelessness.
The very last time I tried to kill
Myself, using a semiautomatic 9 mil.
I chambered a round, aimed right where I think.

The pin fell with the trigger; all I heard was "tink."
I became angry; God couldn't stop me!
I'd chamber one more—I'd make certain I'm free!
For God it's no harder than a thoughtless blink
As I heard another unsuccessful "tink."
Overwhelmed and confused with what I just saw;
I don't know why Papa would choose me at all!
I was terribly sad that He made me stay
In this life of pain and hurtful decay.
Having no choice, I accepted His win,
And never attempted suicide again.

The time came again for what my family did well,
And that was move to a different locale.
Always leaving one job for another
Keeping our family with the perfect cover.
Pig and I moved while mom stayed behind,
To Pennsylvania is where we would find
A house for rent so eventually
Mom could come rejoin the debauchery.

Pig being pig tried one more time
To "please" me at home so I would not find
Anyone to take what I was willing to give;
Pig's certainty grew with a twisted motive
Of what a good father ought to show me,
Please her at home, so she'll not want to be
With anyone else—and no matter what
Pig chose not to listen for his whole heart was fraught
With a thick, black soot and a mind consumed
So those that he "loves" become brutally used.

For the first time, I rebuff his advances,
This cowardly swine would take no more chances.
Finally, Pig with his rather large snout
Said, "I've had enough of you NOW GET OUT!

I hate you, Slut, why can't you see
You are not good enough to live here with me!"

The fear that had kept me enslaved by this monger,
Gave way to fierce anger that made me much stronger.
"You don't want me and I hate to dig!
I think I am the human and you are the pig.
I need to be free and to find my own kind
With my degree in Survival, I'll do just fine!"

With precision and speed I packed what was mine
Into my car, not caring that I
Had no place to go and no one that cared,
But God had a plan that was neatly prepared.
At seventeen I felt worn very thin,
Much later I found Psalm 27:10!

At the time, whatever it was I believed
Didn't matter; it took looking back to perceive
That when I stepped out, or better yet ran,
I did it by faith onto Papa's strong hands.
I always had a place to live,
There was always someone willing to give
Me a job so I could eat;
Granted my life wasn't nice 'n neat,
But it worked...and I got to live
Long enough to see Papa give
Everything David said he saw:
No seed forsaken, no matter how small.
If the only reason I'm still here
Is to make David's point today still clear
Then it is enough; I'm satisfied;
Still learning to walk and to abide
And rest and trust—loving as I go.
Papa wants those like me to know
He's chosen the rejects, the drunks, the whores,

For it is we who confound the self-righteous boars.
For one of God's treasures in life's rehearsal
Is an awesome thing: The Great Reversal.
He takes those unqualified
And succeeds where professionals have tried
And failed. Abraham, a barren soul
Was given a mighty nation's goal.
When he heard God, Noah did not panic—
After all, professionals built the Titanic.
David, the smallest of them all
Got to see Goliath fall.
Ruth by faithfulness would find
She'd made the Messianic line.
Joseph's resumé contained only "slave"
He was not even qualified to save
Himself, but yet at Pharaoh's right hand
He was able to help hungry nations stand.
I could go on, my point remains—
God uses those the world has thrown away.

Up until now I've been talking to all
Who pick up and read this story so small.
Now I address, as only I can
All those who know this trauma firsthand.
For what we've survived and what we've been through,
I dedicate the following poems to you.
They tell their own story of a battered soul
Working too hard to become whole.

I have faced off in ways not so nice,
With each destroyer that's been in my life.
I've completely chopped the family tree,
Divorced and left church on my road to be free.
In all our traumas there remains this truth,
In each of these poems I'm sure you'll find you.
So when you too are finding yourself

Abandoned and orphaned and placed on a shelf
Stop dealing with trauma! Let go of your sin!
Allow God to give you His healing within.

He's taken your beatings, your shame and your pain—
He's taken your weakness; He's changed your name!
You've got a family that's excited to see
What you'll become when you're finally free.
No condemnation! Not one shameful look!
Papa's excited! He knows what it took
For you to arrive at this point alive!
You dared to risk by Faith and try!
He gave you strength that made you say,
    "There's got to be a better way.
Don't know what it looks like or when it will be,
Hold on to me, Papa, as I become me."

The ideas that God through me did express
Hold volumes of Life within hopelessness.
The Holy Spirit, with much urgency,
Would give me these lines of poetry.
Sometimes, like water overflowing a cup,
It was all I could do just to write and keep up!

With Love and Grace I began to ignore
The nasty names of Bitch, Slut and Whore.
My Papa, who longed to keep me from harm,
Patiently urged me to move off the farm.
The energy we can spend on ourselves
As we try on our own to apply James 1:12
Can be wasted if we attempt it alone,
But by the power of Love is easily done;
In turning the tide from what we've been taught
And to stop thinking and living in ways that are not
So lovely and true and are completely against
What Papa believes and what we are meant

To know, to do, to believe and think!
Rest with our Father so when your heart sinks
Into turmoil and doubt, you will KNOW it's not true!
You are so precious He died for you.

2

One of the mainstays of our character
We need to survive that keeps us immature
Is one without God we could never see;
It's a condition called:

Self-Sufficiency

I say I am strong but you will soon see
It's a condition called "self-sufficiency."
Tired of abandonment and a broken heart
I'd rather give up and set myself apart.
I'll take care of my problems after all they are mine.
I won't burden you; I'm fine, no, really, I'm fine.
Having to war with a heart that is split
While longing for others, I'll take care of it.
I'll do it myself, keep muddling through
All the while wishing that someone else knew
The attacks on my heart's vulnerabilities;
I'm eaten up with self-sufficiency.
Like any true victim I'm tired and worn.
I've put up with insaneness I cannot afford.
I'm feeling the strength that I've always had
Slip away while I'm left uncomfortably sad.
Too worn to move forward too lonely to quit;
And again and again, I'm so tired of it.
Today my heart beats as if it's too old.
The fatigue in my bones matches faith that is cold.
My hunger has always compelled me to fight
But this life has left me with no appetite.
The decades of torture, betrayal and abuse
Has caused me to ask more than once, "What's the use?"
How do I risk and humbly receive
And show other people imperfections and needs?
I do not understand how someone so hurt,
Going through life so horribly burnt

Is supposed to heal but continue to risk.
Has God lost his mind? Where is the trick?
As a creature of time, I wait for my queue.
What will it look like? What will He do?

He starts by throwing to the ground;
He knows these strongholds must come down.
There are so many! Most unseen;
The tunnels! The traps! The tricks! The schemes!
"How did THAT get there?" "What do I do?"
The questions are many the answers seem few.
As year after year I end up with less,
Desperation partners with hopelessness.
After all, it is I who do not understand
Nor can I contemplate His plan,
"I'm not even worth it and will never be
Anything more than a failure, you'll see."
Ignoring His mound of complaining dust,
God very lavishly does what He must.
With Wisdom, care and His double-edged sword
He tears down the strongholds and breaks every board.
He does the work and I feel the pain.
He wipes my tears and says, "Please, try again.
This battle's not over it's only begun.
Trust ME, my child, and please do not run.
To see it all now, there'll be no room for Faith.
You WILL see my Glory you WILL have a taste.
I know that all you are able to see
Is the loss you think was created by Me.
I was not the one that created
Your life of pain that inundated
You with failure, fear and doubt;
Watch ME now as I clean it all out!
I'll put your feet on solid ground,
You'll be stronger, I promise and my promise is sound.
I will do what you let ME now please, be still!

I was with you through pain; I honored "free will."
Now you—look at ME and keep your eyes fast
I will uphold your future and bury your past.
This pain will never touch you again.
My Grace will abound and MY WILL, WILL WIN.
These people that used you and left you behind—
I did NOT send them they were NOT Mine!
But if you will let Me, the power of GRACE
Will heal each scar, each pain and each face
And replace them with those that will keep you as dear
As I do. Now rest in My hands, right here."

The Path of Rejection

The Truth will always pull you against the flow;
As you must risk, by Faith, all that you know.
You can honor your father and mother, dear,
But God does make this one thing clear;
When it should stop, when it's time to leave
For a life or spouse with which to cleave.
"Good Christian teaching" may say that you're wrong
When it's GOD taking you away from the throng.
They will teach you and preach you, "The law to obey"
While Grace like a splinter will not go away.
Answer alone to the God who is perfect
And stop being a familial puppet.
If you try to confess, repent and move on
Your divisions and strife will prove it's not gone.
As you work harder to swallow law's pill
You don't get better, only more ill.
For anyone to dare to question the pastor
Is to bring God's wrath and certain disaster.
"Listen, I've studied," he says to impress,
"A fine line splits faith and foolishness!"

Make God alone your only source.
This step alone can change your course
Of what anyone once taught you to do;
STOP your family's control of you.
Their intent may be sincere
But manipulations are never clear.
If they will not respect your space
Manipulation's ugly face
Will be brought out and this will prove
It's not about love, they're controlling you.

So many people proclaim to know
The way each one of us should go.

What it will look like and what it will be
And that God will do predictably
With each of us as He's done through the ages
"Trust me," they gloat, "I have studied the pages."

I have had my Faith snidely mistaken
For rebellion, cowardice or obedience untaken.
God is the One that demands to propose
That He kept me different and only He knows
How He will free me to make me my best.
Most of what's taught is what God is against.
"Forgive me, Oh Lord," my heart fell distraught,
"There is so much programming in what I've been taught.
But if my programming has so much good reason,
Then why am I not yet free from my prison?"
A change of mind's a reject able quest,
As you allow the Spirit to show you what's best.
If they do not want you then don't try to stay.
God's big enough to show you the way.
The Pharisee gutter of "Christian" rejection
Allows for God's Grace and His work of perfection.

This brings me to an eye-opening thought:
All Christ's disciples must have been brought
Up in homes that were dripping with love.
For they thought for themselves, not needing a shove
In the gift of simple trust to obey.
Love casts out fear and says it's okay
To respond to God on your own and leave home;
Wherever He may call you to roam.
Love doesn't control, it sets you free
To be whomever God calls you to be.
Adult kids—here is your wakeup call!
Pleasing parents over God will keep your life small.
You will always find as you walk in Grace
That God will not be second place.

What God taught is so apparent,
He's your ONLY Father, not your foster parent.
He brought you into His family to stay
Moved in and gave you His D.N.A.
Refusing to sever earthly parental connection
Will cause you to live in fear of rejection.
No longer living a life of Faith;
No longer able to have a taste
Of the life and more life He wishes to give
So you can be free and abundantly live.

Galatians 6 down to 13
Talks about those who cannot leave
The control of those given control by law.
Choose not to make your life that small.
A deluge of rejection will hold you fast
To parents and preachers who will not last
And cannot answer to God for you—
Please cut them lose; God told you to.
Anyone or anything
Between you and God will also mean
You are not worthy to follow Christ;
Rejection WAS His earthly strife.

Ephesians 5:1 through 2
Explains what you're supposed to do.
Sit at God's feet to watch and learn
Not follow earthly parental concern.
Parents, like law were given at first
To be the schoolmaster and prove law's curse.
They were never intended to stay in control
And are needless if Love transforms and takes hold.
Parental control, you will soon see,
Will keep you from all God meant you to be.

Christ's first disciples left it all:
Family business and Biblical law,
Without demanding that Christ first prove
And without demanding their families approve
Of His plan for them or His theology;
To hold fast to both, is split loyalty.
At the very least you'll compromise
Or at the worst with God you'll strive.
God won't share you with your family tree,
For He simply stated, "Follow ME."

The Hypocrite

The man who hates fat people while he's a drunk,
The man who hates dirt and smells like a skunk.
He lives in glass houses and throws every stone
He hates his own pain but will break all your bones.
He demands your attention, demands that you see;
While blinded by sins he will never be free.
He curses the dark yet runs from the light.
He hates his own weakness with all of his might.
His heart is all black and his mind is confused
While those that he "loves" become brutally used.
He is a monster a critical abuser
A rapist, a liar and selfish accuser.
Knows nothing of truth but believes he is right
While he rolls in perversion night after night.
He thinks feeling anything makes him insane
So denying everything he becomes inhumane
To life, to love and to anything good;
To become clean he will roll in the mud.
He does not sleep while he wishes for rest
While doing so poorly he's doing his best.
He goes straight through life so aimlessly
All the while wishing so badly to see.

Why do some stay blind and some people see?
Do we choose that way or was it destined to be?
Sometimes we pray and we pray and we pray
But forever and always it seems to stay
Unchanged while others are truly set free
Tell me—
Do we choose that way, or is it destined to be?

Full Affect

Does God really see me?
Does He see me at all?
Have we really lost everything
Because of the fall?

Would Adam have sinned
If he'd been able to see
The affects upon you,
The affects upon me?

I will never know the full effect
Of the choices I make in the things I select
To do, to say, to go and to teach
In the way that I live; all the things that I preach.
The best measure, I think, of what I have given
In truth is what I see in my children.
But even that's tainted if only a tad
By what they will choose, whether good or bad.

Encouragement

It is easy to remember only the bad.
Let's work to remember ALL that you have.
There's so many views in this life that we trod;
Let's see the world according to God:

He is the Victor; His time has not passed.
Our most horrible pains will never last.
Injustices! He has seen every last one—
The ones done to us and the ones we have done.
Knowing what hurts in my life would be,
Required a plan made just for me.
Each of my prayers, both great and small,
As I've learned to wait, He's answered them all.
When pain takes my heart and my words seem to be
Filled with great incredulity
He knows, He carries, He patiently waits
And when I am tired and weary He makes
The sun come again and imparts a new day.
He fills it with mercies and a brand new way
That has flowers and breezes and soft falling rain.
He collects all my tears, understanding my pain.

Sailing Through

Sometimes as we work to be free
We bend to help our family—
Who claim to want the same as you;
We find out later, it's just not true.

I'm in a large boat, can you see?
But I'm not the Captain, oh no! Not me!
I don't know the difference in starboard or port
The masts are too high; I'm too weak and short
To hoist, to pull, to row or steer
So I cannot help you or save you, my dear.
For you are on your ship and I am on mine
And where we end up will be brought out in time.
But I saw you sinking. I thought I could help.
So you came aboard and said that you felt
Thankful, wishing you'd learned out to sail
That you're tired of running around with your pail;
Bailing water only to find that there's more,
Turning your trip of hope into a chore.
The winds have blown and the storms often came
Putting holes in your boat so you often complained.
So with new resolution you took my hand
And agreed that my help was a very good plan;
A new boat, a new course, a new life full of hope—
So why do you stand there missing your boat?

Defective Survivor

As a defective survivor, I hurt like hell.
I'm exhausted from sobbing and simply fell
Crumpled upon the floor in a heap
Soaked from head to toe with grief.
Whose funeral is this that I keep attending
Of wasted years and the tears I've been spending?
I hate the fact that all I can see
Is the defectiveness inside of me.
It's the trauma, the hopeless and unending fray;
The warped thought patterns that won't go away.
For there's been no one, no time and no place
No part of my life I've considered as safe.
Hope was obliterated time and again,
A nightmare from which I could not awaken.
I don't want your sorrow—just your respect.
As my head's been so cloudy I can't see what's next.
One day I'm fine and then again maybe not.
My insides keep getting all tied up in knots.

As I write these words it occurs to me,
Surviving this long, how strong I must be!
Not that I mean in the physical sense
But the hope I've retained in my hopelessness.
To have such strength in the weakest of times;
To risk much love after paying such fines.
To have kept on going when people, for certain
Kept chopping and handicapping my person;
To say, in this life, that has been such a chore
I can't give up now but I'll try just once more.
When the bombs kept exploding, I did not die!
It has stayed within me to say, "I'll try."
I'll work, I'll sweat and there has to be more—
I will respect myself as a survivor!

Whole

I do not know the meaning of "quit"!
Giving up? I'll have no part of it!
In my short life, so far, I've found
By steady Grace I'll hold my ground.
No need to holler, scream or jump
For I'm well braced for things that bump,
In quiet resolve and face like a flint;
Giving up? I'll have no part of it!
In life I may have to dodge and weave,
Or stand my ground as I quietly bleed.
But with Papa I will always, ALWAYS be whole.
For that is the strength Grace gives to my soul.
You can take any part of me you want
You can say what you will, you can tease and taunt
Because I know that I know I'm accepted and whole.
For it is God's Grace permeating my soul.
As I try, as I learn, as I fail and succeed,
You can see in my face that I have no need
Of your crutches, your wheelchairs and handicap spaces!
Take a good look, for the look on my face is
Indicative of the very fact I am whole.
For **that** is the God that lives in my soul.

My Papa

Thank you, Papa, for what you have done.
You kept me from falling when I had to run.
You were my path as I ran through the woods.
When I thought I couldn't, you showed me You would.
As I lived in fear through humanity
You relentlessly prodded, "You can trust Me."
When those that you put in charge of my life
Turned away from me and ignored my strife,
And strangled me with their judgmental noose,
You stood with me as I embraced truth.
I have great respect for what I can't see—
By Grace and trust you live through me.
While others see chance and a boat that's unmanned
With You is a life perfectly planned.
You are Almighty in my classroom of life.
You're the strength of my weakness and Master of strife.
The Light in the darkness the Hanger of Stars,
The Judge of the wicked, the Healer of scars.
While I wait for the day of my final nap,
I'll live by Grace, right here on Your lap.

You

You misunderstood your sin of self-sufficiency for strength—
You confused your desires to do better with envy.
You exchanged safety for control.
You sold respect and bought a whip.
You rejected love and wielded anger.
You mocked mercy and mastered judgment.
You bartered integrity for depravity.
You gave up truth to study lies.
You repeatedly traded your heart for rocks,
Then threw those rocks at me.
The center of your concern,
The center of your world
The center of your love
The center of your thoughts...
Was you.
For all eternity may you understand why...
It was never all about you.

Moving On

Respect what I say or get out of my way—
Moving on.
You can say what you will but with Papa I'm still—
Moving on.
It's a privilege to know me and I say that boldly—
Moving on.
With pain well acquainted; by Grace walk untainted—
Moving on.
To those that abuse, you can keep your excuse—
Moving on.
With Papa and Grace I'm accepted and safe—
Moving on.
Living, believing, accepting, receiving—
Moving on.
The road up ahead may be closed or bulldozed—
Moving on.
No longer rushing with anxieties gushing—
Moving on.
No longer demanding but peacefully standing—
Because I've moved on!

Task Master

If you wish to work harder while not moving faster,
It's as easy as this: let fear be your master!

Another Goodbye

My heart being guided by wisdom and care,
With God-given freedom I pointedly stare
And am lead to face off with every abuser—
Even the "loving" manipulative users.
His perfect love will cast out and disgrace
Every offender that keeps their place
In my life through my family tree;
Offenders must go; I will be free.
I'll have my funerals and do what I must
As I walk by faith and dare to trust.
As freedom reigns, my view becomes bright
As Grace settles in to finish my fight.
The same God that watched my horrible fate
By Grace restores what the locusts ate.
To embrace this change I can no longer hold
To people and teachings I regarded as gold.
I will finally receive and proclaim what I've learned:
It is NEVER okay to watch me burn!
I'd just blame my dad, but the only catch is
I see that my mom is holding the matches.
My dad had the plan and the gasoline,
He struck the match so it would seem
It's all on him, but yet there's another—
It's time to admit that it was my mother.

Another relationship must die;
And the funeral where I will say "Good-bye"
Will be kept in a plot very close to the other;
Next to my Father is buried my Mother.

Good-bye Mom.

Forever

My life being built on fear and betrayal
Makes it easy to see I've been set up to fail.
To work off a blueprint put there by a louse,
Truly ensured that I'd pick the wrong spouse.
But even then God will work to protect
The union of marriage He holds with respect.
It takes two people to make strong and sound,
But sadly takes one to tear it all down.

I dreamt of forever, but at what cost?
At what time and when do you say, "All is lost?"
I worked, I churched, I read, I prayed;
It got too expensive, the price that I paid.
I counseled, I talked, I waited, I begged,
It's no use, I called it; it's dead.
I went bankrupt trying to be
Whatever it was that you asked of me.
Constantly playing the dutiful wife
By giving up with each encounter of strife.
I worked way too hard seeking my part,
Knowing this mess was dead from the start.
I didn't love you and you didn't care.
You wanted a pretty face in a wheelchair.
You wanted a project, although that's not wrong,
You failed to change when this "project" got strong.
As I changed, your response in kind,
Should be a marriage redefined.
Believing you were perfect, you simply stayed,
Refusing to change the life that we'd made.
As I posed the question of what I should do,
Your response with a chuckle, "I don't want you."
There would be no counselor. You saw no need.
"You knew what you got when you married me.
I'm the same person I was long ago,

There's nothing wrong with me, I know!"
You followed up with this well-placed kick,
"Let me know when you get yourself fixed."

I guess the last funeral that I must attend,
Is the one where my "forever heart" mends.
Letting go of the promise, forgiving betrayal,
Throwing it on my pile marked "fail."
I wanted to keep you, if only a dream
But the drama went bad and ended the scene.
Reality: relentless, untimely and cruel
Continuously stomped me and made me a fool.

As funeral directors, my Papa's the best.
The plot is as far as the East from the West.
The viewing is private, the service discreet,
At the end, I lay the bill at His feet.

Just Live

Ponder, question, work and give!
But when, oh when will I just get to live?
How do I plot a course that is mine?
Screwed up again! Try one more time!
By "acceptance addiction" I pour every part
Of my mind, my soul, my body and heart
Into each person I am trusting to be
The one who will give back to me.
With unsafe boundaries I'm seeking connection
Leaving my heart without ample protection.
I continue to work, and I work for free.
Giving too much in hopes you'll love me.

Manipulation in all of its forms
Whether guilt trips in words, smiles or charms
Is used as I try to guarantee
That the end result will finally be
So perfect and lovely; I'm so in control,
While each one involved is so miserable.
Security bound in selfishness
Is a lie, an illusion and an empty promise.
I'll wear my mask so no one will see
That I want things to be the way I want them to be!

Once again I can only stand and stare
At the mess I have made as I try to compare
The components of each time I work so hard,
To be used—left blackened and charred.
When will I stop this? When will I learn?
It's NEVER okay to watch me burn!
Whether the "watcher" is you or is me,
This can't go on! I want to be free!
Things will get better! I wish something would give!
I sure wish I knew how to just live.

Passport Problem

I don't want to be you. I want to be me.
But there's a problem with my identity.
My papers have been falsified so far
That I don't even know where the originals are!
The picture's correct. The dates are too.
But the information's not me; it's you!
With my programming I always decide
To try to be "you" while the "me" hides.

With laser precision I've trained hard to be
What everyone wants or needs of me.
My role to please, I learned so well
'Cause it's all about you, couldn't you tell?
To ensure my protection along with your smile
I'd read all the tacit! Go the extra mile!
The conduct I learned to ensure I'd survive
Is killing me now as I struggle and strive.

I know it will seem that my passport's in order
Until my judges begin to look closer.
Maybe someday there will no longer be
A problem with my identity.
Pictures, info—one day the whole batch
Will be arranged to completely match!
What is that like? Tell me, when will it be,
That I will just live and finally be me!

Amen and *GLORY* with fresh revelation
Comes life giving hope and a redefined station!
Within my answer I found my place.
He called to me in the teaching of Grace!
I was made weak by one man's rejection—
And I was made whole by One Man's acceptance!
Papa with love from the throne room kept calling,

"I can't," I wept, "I'm so appalling!
I know You still love me (with every flaw)
But I can't even keep just one of the law!"

The sad truth was I had lost the taste
Of a beautiful thing called "childlike faith."
As I stood crying—could I really lay down
The idea I didn't belong with the Crowned?
I truly believed that I was to blame
As I heard the words, "He bore your shame!"
I needed to see Him both willing and strong
That His Son is the reason *why* I belonged!
He came for me once as He hung there and died,
He calls for me twice through Grace to abide!
I had laid down *my* sin to be set me free,
But what about the sins inflicted on me?

Running to Papa required a clear
Belief that He actually wanted me there.
The sins that were done to me were so vast,
I could only believe that I'd been outcast.
But, He kept calling, dispelling rejection.
The look on His face was steadfast affection.
He called me "spotless," but I must confess
All I could see was a tattered mess.
My clothing was dirty and badly worn
For the sin of this world left me battered and torn.
"The dirt," He said, "on your clothes that you see,
Doesn't belong to you, it belongs to Me!!
I not only took what you do,
But also took what was done to you!"
As His words began to sink in,
Hope spoke to my soul, "You know He'll win!"
As a child determined I stuck out my chest,
Balled up my fists, took a deep breath
And mustered the courage it would take to believe,

Closed my eyes and RAN as the truth was received.
Daddy had waited my entire life
To scoop me up and heal this strife!
He did it, too, as we swung 'round;
I became whole, safe and sound.
No longer rejected, no longer alone—
My heart was now full with the fact I'd come home.

A few more thoughts before I go,
There's a few more things God wants you to know.

One of the things that I thought was unique
Was that going to church helped keep me weak.
Every time I'd believe that God was so good
I'd go back to church believing I would
Find many others who trusted the same.
But it wasn't long before I came
To this bizarre and sad conclusion:
Church, for me, was a nice-looking prison.

In each sermon were so many "shoulds"
Reinforcing that I was just damaged goods!
"For crying out loud! I don't need you
To tell me what I already knew!
This world has already beaten me down
From "King's Kid to court jester and clown!
I don't need your help, in God's gracious court
To remind me of just how much I've fallen short!"
If abundant living and being free
After salvation is all up to me,
Then I'll walk away and only confess
You've left me with even more hopelessness.

But when I was alone and it was just me
And God spending time on my balcony,
I was okay, our rapport just fine!

I could believe God was good and kind.
The Holy Spirit knowing what to do,
Would remind me of a girl made new.

I could not stop how church made me feel,
On an unacceptable "hamster wheel"
Of being "okay," but then again maybe not—
Going back and forth—you can keep the whole lot!
I surrendered and believed I was too weak to be
A part of any church family.

Then one day, as I said before
I learned of a place that taught much more
Than rules and laws and "missing the mark!"
God was excited to light up my dark
And hopeless path I had been set on!
In learning of Grace, I found a new dawn.
It took many months to complete this new lesson,
'Twas not the church that was ever my prison
But what was taught from the pulpit, so bold.
You're only "okay" if you do what you're told.

It's easy to spot those who think they're so great,
You'll find them with signs—spreading the hate.
They pound on their pulpits, they scream and they shout,
They know nothing of Love and forgot all about
The fact that if God took *their* hearts on parade,
Their hatred for others would certainly fade!
With brand new humility and in total loss,
They'd find many friends at the foot of the cross.

If anything preached is performance based
Then the pastor and people will take God's place.
Their acceptance now being paramount
To ensure your heavenly treasure count.
Have you prayed today? Have you told any lies?

Have you crossed all your *t*'s and dotted all *I*'s?
Before your pastor allows you some ease
He must stir things up with the next series.

Following rules shows a lack of trust
That you, not God, do what you must.
I have lived far too long in a self-righteous hex.
It's a spiritual game of Russian roulette.
"Law seeds" don't allow for true inner change—
The only difference between "lost" and "saved."
But what seed *is* sown should be very clear
For the flower that blooms by control is FEAR.
Control and Law seem reasonable
For without them chaos seems inevitable.
But what you may be fixing to do
Is join in the chorus of Matthew 7:22!
I shake my head as I think of the shock
These people in Matthew were in—quite a lot!
God makes it plain, they were in much surprise
Of their true eternal reward when they died.

Those that are orphaned and have no place,
Will find what you need in the teaching of Grace.
Not some Grace mixed in with Law—
But Grace alone; Grace as ALL!!

Grace, a well-kept flowerbed
Does not need law, like weeds, to spread
And take the place through Grace you keep,
In Papa's protection, love and peace.

Sincere Praise to God above,
For those who preach God's Grace and Love!
Embrace "I CAN'T" and fall diminished,
Yet completely whole in: IT IS FINISHED!

Part Two

T. L. Jones the Rookie:

Papa Shines in the Darkest of Places

Chapter One

There are times when God steps in and stops someone from an action. There are other times when He intervenes and keeps us from the end result. Although keeping us from the end result may be the only supernatural thing we see, both interventions are equally miraculous. I have lived long enough to understand that Papa has intervened in my life using both of those tactics. I've been able to look back on many events in my life and not be able to account for sudden turns or outcomes.

I've been suicidal and I've given up. There is a difference. If you're suicidal, you're still trying to end some vicious cycle of hurt. If you've given up, you're not trying to do anything at all. Either one can be with or without hope. That may sound strange, but think about it for a bit. People don't want to die—they want the pain to end, and they want the cycle broken. Ending your life may appear to be the only way to stop things or keep things from happening, but it isn't. I've written my story and talk to others to prove that very point. As an LEO (law enforcement officer), the suicide calls I went on all contained evidence that the person who attempted suicide had an "Oh, shit" moment before they slipped into unconsciousness. That was the term we used to describe that very moment when it occurred to the victim that they really did not want to die; when their impending demise was so real they involuntarily left behind evidence of the fact that all they wished to do was live. Sadly, some realized that at the point of no return.

Why did Papa spare me? Why does Papa spare anyone? There isn't *one* answer...there are many. *Three times!* What I did *should have worked!* Three times, I was completely angry that it did not. I remember each episode when I decided it was going to be the day my pain was going to end, and I had made a plan. My spirits were always lifted; I was in a fantastic mood that whole day because I was finally going to be free. My friend, sadly enough, that's when it's real.

I remember bouncing home off the bus. I plopped my book bag down and carefully unwrapped the handful mixture of pills I had bought from a "friend" at school. I had done my research; this was going to work. My parents (probably my mom) would find the body the next morning when she would notice I did not get up for school. The thought of her finding me made my heart light as a feather—it wasn't about her or how she felt or anyone else...I was going to be free. I threw the pills down my throat, gracefully assembled myself on my bed with my hands folded across my stomach (not to be morbid, I actually did find that position most comfortable), and went to sleep. I remember smiling. Then...I woke up the next morning absolutely pissed off. I was fifteen years old—or was it thirteen?—and I always feel like I'm lying, but the truth is when your life only knows this level of chaos, events, and dates get terribly jumbled. *So much happens* it's impossible to keep it all straight.

I was thrown out of the house when I was seventeen because I refused to cooperate with my earthly dad's intent to "be a good father." I had a job and Papa found me a wonderful little efficiency apartment to live in. However, Christmas was coming, and, as we all know, it's also the suicide season. As I worked in my cubicle that day, the decision and plan was made, and I acquired a bottle of 100-proof whisky and a new box of razor blades. Believe it or not, my parents actually expected a visit on Christmas Day. But why shouldn't they? I *never* disappointed them. (I say that with brand new resolve actually.) Once again, my heart was light as a feather. Christmas day may come and go and a couple of days may have to slide by before they actually come and *look* for me and not simply think I'm just in one of my "moods." But it would happen sooner or later. Hell, I didn't care if it had to go far enough along to make the landlord stop by for not getting the rent or for someone to complain about the smell.

I went home, undressed, got in the tub, put the headphones on, and started drinking. When I was too numb to care, I took the razor blade and made a nice deep cut in my wrist area. The new razor made it a breeze, and the lack of pain response because of the alcohol made it easier to bear up and keep going without hesitation. Honestly, until after the cut was completed, I virtually felt nothing at all; that's exactly how I wanted it. Afterward, I just continued to drink. I was going to go until I passed out from the alcohol or from the bleed out; I didn't care which. I woke up the next morning *pissed as hell!* There was no cut, no scar, and not even a stupid hangover! I just stomped around being pissed at the mess I had to clean up. The tub and myself were covered in blood. And you know what I *never did?* Well, I certainly didn't "thank God" (I yelled at Him and cussed Him), but I never thought to compare this with the last time and *understand* the miracle that had taken place not once but twice. I didn't see this as a miracle at all or as a testimony of His great and wonderful LOVE—it was Papa's punishment. From my perspective, if He loved me, He would let me die because He knew how much pain I was in. But since He wouldn't let me die, His desire must be to keep me *in pain*. I used these two deliverances as proof that not only was I a horrible person but I had also unwittingly signed up to be the "whipping boy" God apparently needed. I shake my head now. Just how freakishly warped is that! Very. But it was my truth. It was how I was raised, like so many others.

Sometime later, I moved back home. I believe it was to go to college or because I was in college—not sure, again, with the jumbled time line. Being home was just as much of a pain as living on my own. I was hurting either way. During this time, I put up with my "father" talking to me about all the women he screwed while in the Navy, how he missed them, and how fat my mom was. I also had to live with being accused of screwing everyone, being a whore (which, as far as he was concerned, was the only reason I did something bizarre, like go to the movies or have a boyfriend), and not respecting his "rules." At one point, he said something to both my mother and I about being lesbians (yep, a real winner). He always said he would charge me rent, until one day I shot back, "I wish you would. If you remember, I offered you rent and you thought it was despicable that I would purpose such a thing—you know, with you being my parent and all. I'll gladly pay you rent to shut you up." If he had taught me to be anything I could dress up to be remotely positive, it was to be responsible for everything...to a fault.

My final episode was while I was enduring my home life once again. I had a semiautomatic 9 mil. I was familiar with weapons, and I still like the way a pistol looks. I was going to kill myself; this time, I was gonna be proper about it. You can see the "step up" here, can't you? You see, the first time—maybe I got the concoction wrong, maybe that's why it failed. The second time—maybe I got drunker than I thought and imagined things. (You can really talk yourself into or out of anything.) This time, I am leaving nothing to chance or imagination. To ensure the pistol had a round ready to fire, I emptied the magazine, locked the slide back, and inserted one. Releasing the slide forward meant it was ready to fire. The safety was off. This time was a little different. There was no lightheartedness. There was no peace or thoughts of freedom.

As I look back, there was more vengeance and hate. My freedom was just an awesome by-product. I'll make sure they had a mess to clean up. I wanted no hesitations. I was going to be free. In one clean motion, I put the pistol to my temple and pulled the trigger as soon as the cool metal registered on my skin…"tink." Nothing. I took advantage and rode the wave of my exploding anger, and with a practiced graced, I pulled the slide back, the shell ejected, and, in its place, a fresh round. I let the slide go, put it to my temple, and pulled the trigger a second time…"tink." I've never studied it, but I do believe an expert on the physical side of this episode would back up the fact that I probably passed out from the emotional traumas and struggles all maxed out at once. The mixture of all-consuming fear, anger, and rage, along with every ounce of "what the hell just happened," were intense.

I woke up on my bed with my pistol loosely held in my palm. This time I wasn't pissed. I was sincerely defeated—all the way to my core. I submitted to Papa's punishment and believed He was going to intervene for the rest of my life to keep me in my earthly hell. Something that amazes me to this day is the fact that when I listen to other women/teens talk about similar situations of abuse, there was *always* a time when they woke up to some degree and thought, "I'm not wrong, you are!" My question remains: why did I not do that while growing up…ever? That bothers me. If the answer is unimportant to this life, Papa will take care of it—either way, I'm good.

People caught up in these abusive patterns have been trained to be shortsighted and rely only upon themselves (hence, the poem self-sufficiency). Unfortunately, they very rarely come to realize they let themselves down by the patterns they are trapped in, and they constantly land in much the same situations they run from—over and over. Men included. These patterns are twofold: one, they have absolutely NO CLUE about Papa's LOVE for them or their own value; two, their "picker is broke." They constantly pick people who

AGREE with their perspective of their own value. If anyone will let Papa change how they see themselves, their pickers would get "unstuck," and even their choices in friends and jobs will change. Right believing LEADS to right living. We don't have a hard time understanding the fact that when someone thinks they're ugly, they also make bad clothing and hairstyle choices. When someone believes they are beautiful and worthwhile, their clothing and hairstyles/color reflects that belief—SAME THING!

When I divorced, I knew my picker was broke. If I did not take the years needed to let Papa change me, then divorce was not going to fix anything. I needed a new "picker"; I needed to view myself differently. What gets in the way of waiting on this change is the "acceptance addiction" adult survivors of abuse ALWAYS have...MEN INCLUDED. Someone else gives them their value. If you don't know if this is you, ask yourself this question: Are you okay (valuable/happy/content) being alone? I didn't ask if you wanted to be alone for the rest of your life; there's a difference. With no one in our lives, we believe we're worthless. I did the same dumb thing. Papa did use that, though. From the time I started dating again and throughout the four years it took to meet my husband, my choices got much, much better—person after person. That was an encouragement to my soul.

I had no idea that when I tried to die for the last time, my future as an LEO would give me the privilege to prove to so many people caught up in the patterns of abuse that there is HOPE. If you will be patient and live, you will get to find out how Papa will use you. I didn't know about this book. I didn't know anything, except extreme decision making from a life lived in survival mode. I didn't know that at forty years old, I would get to tell people from five years old up to those in their eighties that no matter where you've come from, THERE IS HOPE. As an LEO, I'll never forget the faces of those I found in abusive distress, especially those who lived lives that mirrored my own. When the wisdom I had been privileged to gain was coupled with Papa's leadership, some very supernatural things took place. Even in the dead of night from 2200 – 0600 hours (10:00 PM – 6:00 AM), Papa was actively working in the lives of those who believed they were forgotten and doomed. The following true stories are proof of HOPE and are demonstrative of the fact that Papa still sees our very hearts and wants like crazy to intervene and wrap His arms around us. He used me many times, and I LOVED it. As I reminisce about my experience as an LEO and miss it terribly, I must admit I believe I miss being a part of that supernatural way I got to help those in crisis more than the job itself. Without Papa's interventions, each call would have probably just been a "job." How sad.

Chapter Two

A call I was dispatched to lead me in the path of the life of a fifteen-year-old boy. I got on scene, and, as usual, within minutes (which after some experience this turned into seconds) I had the abusers, codependents, and victims sized up. Papa, through the Holy Spirit, was faithful to point out even the smallest details tucked away in their demeanor (the tacit communication of body language, sentence structure, and tone) that gave me much needed wisdom on how to proceed with each call. By analyzing each person's behavior, accusations, and responses, I was usually able to get a pretty decent feel for what kind of families and abuses each one had come from and what kind of behaviors they were engaging in now with each other, no matter what they were saying.

On this particular call, the father was definitely the abuser, and Papa was jumping up and down in my spirit in a way that led me to believe I was going to see something extremely amazing. After the father was done going off about how his son was so stupid and that he wanted the State to raise him and wanted him off his property, I asked the second officer to keep the parents in the living room and asked the parents' permission to speak to the young man privately. This separation is harder to achieve when the parents actually care, but with the undeserving parent, it's easy—for they want someone to "straighten their kid out" anyway. For me, it was so stinking easy to promise I'm going to "straighten them out," because I actually cared; you can't help but respond to Papa's love. They wholeheartedly agreed.

I took him back to his room and very quietly asked him to sit. He behaved as though I was just another adult ready to give him some sort of tongue-lashing—just another lecture full of all the things he ought to be doing or ought not. I stooped down and got eye level with him. The Holy Spirit was *very* strong, and I was terribly excited to see this boy's reaction, for even I really didn't know what I was going to say or do from one second to the next. I was literally allowing Papa to lead every word. It's really cool, for I am just as much of a spectator as anyone else—it's exciting.

I said, "Roll up your sleeve." The silence changed. The energy in the room was incredible. The look on the boy's face was complete awe. I smiled (I couldn't help it). God really wanted to do something in this boy's life, and I *knew* where He was headed with this. I repeated my request and added, "I know what you've been doing."

At fifteen, this boy was big enough to give his daddy a run for his money. Yet with each blazing cut down his dad leveled in our presence, all he did was shrink further and further inward. As I listened to the dad, Papa spoke very clearly: "You know what this means." (He was talking about the boy.) I got the strong sense that although the words hurt, the boy on the inside was *agreeing* with his dad. I know what I did when I agreed with my "rented parent" that I was not worth the skin draped over my own body. I had ways of punishing myself. I believed Papa was making it clear to me that this boy was engaged in that same type of self-punishment.

As he rolled up his sleeve, slash marks became visible. He was a cutter. The level of awe on the boy's face told me that not only was he surprised I knew (as it was never mentioned), but it was also something no one else knew about either.

There were fresh slashes and a couple that were a few days old. I didn't examine them—that wasn't the point. With all the love Papa had for him and all the hurt I knew he was going through, I told him about myself and my own past with cutting, and I told him why we do it. I was the same age when I cut on myself, and, along with giving him my age, I verified the shortsightedness of it all. I am proof there is HOPE. I told him to hold on, to expose himself to as many positive people as he could. If he would hold onto HOPE, he was going to make it. I wanted him to know he did not have to be like "them" (motioning to his parents), and when he got to make his own choices, he should learn from those who have succeeded because his present role models (again motioning to his parents), for now, were lame and wrong in their assessment of his value. I encouraged him to obey as best as he could, and when he became his own man, he should leave and never look back. I told him to keep his eyes fixed on his future, *not* his past, and to please call me at the PD if he needed anything. It may be semantics, but I *did* "straighten him out!" Ha! He wasn't smiling, but he was at peace. There are certain addresses as an LEO you get to memorize. They just can't seem to stop the stupidity. This address was one of them. The final touch to this Amazing Grace encounter was this: we never went to that address again.

Chapter Three

Emergency counseling 101! That was most of my job actually. Trying to straighten people out in "twenty minutes or
less" is no easy task, but with Papa, I know I left many people
much better off than when I found them...except this once.

We never saw it coming. There are just some things you
are not going to fix. If someone has truly made up his or her
mind to commit suicide, you'll never know about it. You'll
never know until someone finds the body. The next story is
a memorial to a man who did not get to change his mind. I
almost feel as though it is my privileged obligation to remember him here, for I truly don't think he has anyone else
to do so.

He was in his late thirties, maybe early forties. It was
about 0300 hours (3:00 AM), and he was crying while wan-
dering the streets. He was not being careful with his footing
as he walked, so someone called 911, believing him to be in-
toxicated. My "brother in blue" (he was also a brother in
Christ; we will call him Jack) and I got out with him and
began to question him. Our first priority was to ascertain
whether his apparent distress was due to any physical injury. Then we needed to find out if he was under the influence of anything (including prescription medications) that

might render him too impaired to be safely under the control of his actions in public. We had found him at the end of a long series of life's letdowns. Now, the final blow was that his girlfriend had just changed his address to the city streets. He said he had no one to call; that there was no one left in his life who cared. We hear that a lot; only to watch them turn around in about fifteen minutes and call mom to come get them. Understandably so, even though we didn't completely disregard that statement when he first laid it out there, we held it suspect as we continued to question him in an effort to best help him.

By golly! This man had no one, not even an acquaintance. His story and hurts checked out. We offered him a ride to somewhere safe—anywhere. He assured us that if we could get him to the city limits he would be safe because where he stayed was not too far from there. He gave us the name of the complex where he stayed, and we were familiar with it. An undesirable location for sure, but close to where we could take him. We double-checked his personal info (standard procedure—don't want to help a fleeing felon now, do we), and he assured us he would be okay if we could simply get him most of the way. He was not drunk; he was not under the influence of any impairing substance as best as we could tell, and once he calmed down and got most of his crying out of his system, he made perfect sense. We followed protocol and got permission to transport him to his desired location. We did. Jack took him, dropped him off, and hung out long enough to be satisfied that everything would go as well as we had it planned in our heads. About an hour and a half later, we found his remains dusted across the hood and side of a car parked in our district. After he was dropped off and Jack was out of sight, he sat down in the middle of the darkened highway, crossed his legs, lowered his head, and simply waited to die. The driver of the vehicle, being only about nineteen, got a shock coming out of that dark curve—one he may need some counseling to get over.

Jack called me later the next day and asked, as any human being who truly cared would: "What did we miss? Did we really do all we could?" It actually touched my heart greatly that he called and demonstrated his love for a fellow human being. It also stirred up my own hurt over this loss of life. I hadn't really stopped long enough to admit the fact that I needed a small cry—just to let it go. I told Jack that I believed if there would have been anything at all that Papa had wanted us to see or do to intervene, we would have known. I told Jack to look at it this way (these words were Papa's doing for sure)—this man's tragic life is now at peace, and Papa agreed with him it was time for his pain to end in this way. Honestly, it was the most loving response you could possibly have over this. There is no answer as to why things turn out the way they do, but I know this: Papa's great LOVE and awesome wisdom provides us with His best solution for the greatest amount of people for the longest amount of time about anything. God is into love; He is not into punishment—we do bad quite well on our own. The enemy comes to kill, steal, and destroy; he cannot create, give, or build.

All LEOs are taught you cannot take these calls with you. You cannot take eight hours of dealing with the end result of people's problems to heart. My high-octane counterparts interpreted that to mean, "don't care." With any concept you can stop too short or go too far, it's called being unbalanced, and most people lack appropriate boundaries. I had already had my fill of solving other people's problems as a codependent teen and through my twenties. I wore myself flat out running to the rescue of others. By the time I became an LEO, I knew better, and I knew the difference between serving with honor and excellence and being sucked dry and used. So my perspective was, I thought, very balanced: while on scene, give it all you got; when it's done, you walk away as if it never happened. The fact that I hurt for this man simply meant I was human, and I hadn't lost that aspect—that's a good thing. Occasionally, at the end of a call or shift, I would endure the brotherly teasing of my counterparts at the fact that I actually had feelings and were dealing with them. If they wanted to end up a mess after twenty plus years of dealing with the mess of others, they were welcome to it. I'll deal with my baggage now, thanks.

Chapter Four

I believe that the Bible teaches us plainly what psychology claims to have proven: a man (talking about people in general) cannot help but display who he is, no matter what he claims. He will give himself away if there is anyone capable of listening, for as a man thinks in his heart...*so is he*. That is the person I seek out when dealing with others—who they *are*, who their heart is giving them away to be—not who they *claim* to be. They will match up or not. Mostly not.

Papa was always willing and able to show up and show off! I was able to deal with the public with more than just popular talk-show psychology. Oftentimes, whatever they were actually spouting on about was not the real problem anyway—just the present splinter. Many times Papa would actually lead me to completely different topics than what they were going on about. Every time He did that, the questions I would be able to ask would cut to far deeper matters, so we could dispense with the whining and sobbing at hand (over which I could do nothing). And if they were willing, we could get onto changes that *matter*. Once I could see where Papa was going, I could keep the subject on task so I could do the most service in the shortest amount of time, because far too often, there were calls holding.

A twenty-five-year-old female had called very late one night to keep her husband from killing her. I forgot the particulars, but she said something that Papa grabbed hold of and dangled in front of my face. I was actually picking up things from her body language and familiarity with not just abuse but sexual abuse. She paused to take a breath from describing her present dilemma, and I cut in, "Wait. Please, if I may," and I motioned for her to step further away from earshot of others to a more private area of her yard. "I have to ask, who sexually abused you growing up, your mom or your dad? 'Cause I'm confused." She hadn't been speaking of that at all. (Now, before you go and think I ran around playing "Dr. Phil" when there were serious laws broken—it wasn't like that at all. The only time Papa led me to deviate in such manners was because it was very appropriate and extremely healthy for the outcome of the person and the call.)

I have noticed that in dealing with adult children of abuse, the types of abuses they're familiar with will be found in the way they communicate their comfort or discomfort with a particular abuse. For example: she was comfortable with sexual abuse but hysterical over him laying hands on her (uncomfortable with physical abuse). With Papa's help, I could pick up these pieces and deal with people on a whole different level.

Upon being asked the question, she fell to wondering silence, but most importantly, she now *believed* in not just a casual way on what I said shortly after my arrival—that I understood where she was coming from for real. I knew that usually, when I would say that on scene, the broken people would shrug it off as if it was something I'm supposed to say. When Papa gave me what I needed to stop her in her tracks, she now knew, in a supernatural way, that someone actually *did know* and care. Hope makes all the difference in the world. Because of our connection (or through me, her connection with a God who really loved her), she took my advise on domestic violence seriously. Not like a cop reading from a pamphlet, she hung on my every word like I actually knew what to do. Turns out, when she was six, her mother began selling her into sexual slavery for her drug fixes. Using common vocabulary and body language on such a horrifying topic makes sense once you know why. By the way, we never went to that address again either. *Papa is amazing.*

Hope was my point. It was always my point, and that tone got set early on. My very first call after being cut loose on third shift to work alone was the rape of a five-year-old little girl by the mother's live-in boyfriend. It might stand to reason, given my background, that I should have a problem with objectivity or emotion on this call. Strangely enough, it energized me. In the academy, they taught us that no matter who you are, there will be that one call you can't shake but will shake you. So, it left me logically wondering how I would respond to a call like this. I had two solid objectives going in. First, to build an objective and airtight case, and second, if time and conversation permitted, be a proof that there is life with hope after anything. My first objective was met with the drug-impaired coward being chased, caught, arrested, and confessed before I left. The second objective, although without the same finesse I found later, was also met. The mother kept grabbing, holding, and crying over her daughter, wailing, "Oh, my baby! What are we gonna do?" I had to find a polite way to get her to listen. How do you kindly cut in on a mother's hysterics? Sadly, you can't. Sometimes you have to appear cruel. I ended up "pulling rank" (as I call it) and pretty much demanding she stop. The little girl was trying to play with her bear and showed me her toys. She was trying to be "normal" already. The mother was the problem. I could see the "victim mentality" this little girl would never escape if her mom didn't get a grip. Once she quieted, I simply informed her to LOOK at her daughter now—on the path to normal already, and she had the choice of keeping her a victim. I shortened it up for you—I think you get it. The mother's communication, both tacit and verbal, seemed to indicate we were on the same page when I left. The little girl gave me one of her glass marbles. I carried it with me every night and still have it to this day. Every time I felt it in my pocket, I remembered her and prayed for her. There is HOPE.

My first love on this job, if you can't tell, is instilling hope in the hopeless. But Papa did a good job in giving me wisdom on a wide range of people. It's so simple and amazingly accurate, and it started with raising two boys. The more honestly you know yourself, the better and more wisely you can deal with others. The simple philosophy I used on my boys worked on the streets as well. I extended mercy to all with my guard up. Prove me right that this mercy is what you need. If they (my boys or those I dealt with in an official capacity) proved me right, I did not eat crow, arrest someone needlessly, write a bad ticket, or make a bad case. However, if they proved me wrong, your one chance was used up, and I would haul ass in the opposite direction. You were going to get what you needed if I showed up—help, to jail or to safety. It worked. It is good (and sometimes difficult) to care more for the public than your own ego, but it can keep you out of a lot of trouble in the long run.

Lord knows, as an LEO, you have very few friends. It was cool at first as a rookie when my girlfriends would introduce me as "the cop." It didn't take long, though. Just after a time or two, I quickly realized my name became "Cop." Even if my name had been mentioned on the intro, it was very quickly lost as soon as my career choice was stated. So, I insisted very sternly and up front that my career be left out. When asked, I simply stated I worked for the city. At five feet three inches and a hundred and twenty pounds, an LEO was the last thing they would think of until they got to know me. LEOs aren't made, they're born. You either own the ground you walk on or you don't. No one can give that to you; it's the attitude in everyday life that has people betting on you in the fight even when you're the small one. An LEO, by presence alone, can control the behavior of up to six people at one time. Without this attitude, you are not only useless but a liability to those you serve with.

Chapter Five

The people in my town were pampered. So much so that even though our city was growing by leaps and bounds, there were still enough elderly citizens, who grew up with the leaders of our PD, who still thought it was Mayberry. One night, right before shift change, about a half dozen radios in the work area lit up with a 911 dispatcher who hated like mad what she had to say (the subtleties you could not detect as a rookie were very apparent after some experience). An elderly woman, at about 2130 hours (9:30 PM), needed help (long pause from the dispatcher) changing her vacuum cleaner bag. Another had a raccoon in her house. Some laughed their butts off while others cursed the idea that the PD still had to answer those types of calls. We went and helped change her cleaner bag, and, as usual, we were offered cookies to show their appreciation while we listened to them walk down memory lane.

In defense of those who hated those types of calls, it wasn't that we didn't like taking those "Boy Scout" jobs, it was the fact that we knew we had to answer *any* calls, no matter how ridiculous, in the order they were received, not according to importance. So, if the vacuum cleaner call came in before the call for help in an assault, we had to change the bag before we could save a life. I tried to be involved with as many "Boy Scout" calls as any other call, including asking those who were walking on the side of the road if they needed a ride somewhere (on a very dull night). I enjoyed helping people with no strings attached. For some, it helped them with their view of LEOs—we were not only here to put people in jail.

The pampered people of our city called 911 about *everything*. Types of calls that I started out hating but grew to enjoy were calls against groups of juveniles. These were calls put in by people who, upon seeing a group of "juveniles" in a parking lot somewhere, were absolutely convinced they were up to no good (welcome to the "Bible Belt"). The first few times I came upon such peaceful gatherings, it was a little turbulent. As I approached them, they were extremely defensive. Papa enabled me to interpret this behavior to indicate not who they were but how they were used to being treated by not only the adults but also by LEOs. They weren't doing anything wrong. In the majority of cases, they weren't juveniles at all but were eighteen to twenty-three years old, and it was obvious (to me anyway) that they were just hanging out or skate boarding and were not harmful to anyone or anything. A few of the shop owners had complained from time to time about the litter they would leave, so after I gained their respect, I offered a solution. Since every group denied being the litter offenders, I always approached them as if they were totally innocent but suggested that if each one would simply pick up one piece and leave the area better than they found it, the shop owners would beg them to hang out there. I actually saw it happen, too, without them knowing. It didn't take long. I never worked to be popular with them but it happened.

I treated them with respect, with the same philosophy Papa gave me to raise my boys: you're a human being first, under my authority second. I'll only "pull rank" on you if you force me to. That is simple and amazingly effective. People have a tendency to live up to the standard you draw them into, not push, pull, or shove them into. One night, I got a pleasant surprise. I was getting out of my car on a group juvenile call, and I heard this proclamation, *"Great! I told you somebody was going to call the cops!"* Another distant voice cut in and said, "No! No! Shut up! It's the chic cop. No man, she's cool! She'll listen." It was a very busy night, so I was in a mental rush and that stopped me in my head. I allowed it to register. I felt privileged to have their voluntary respect, and I had just gotten reminded to slow down and make sure I kept it. They were going to rely on the name I had built for myself for being consistently fair and respectful. Pretty awesome considering how I used to see juveniles.

This was an age group I had feared and even hated for most of my life. I pretty much regarded them like everyone else did—a group we had to "put up with until they grow up." But since my boys were now teens and we were privileged to live in a home of mutual respect, I had come to understand this group and feel for them. They can smell bullshit and hypocrisy a mile away. They can smell fake like a shark can smell blood. Their one major downfall, due to their shortsightedness from a lack of experience, is they are incredibly judgmental and without mercy—the same mercy they wished others had for them. As my boys grow, I am painfully aware that this age group is without mercy, because they are treated without mercy and therefore have no one, on this particular issue, they can lean on to learn from. If they don't respect you and you have not proven yourself trustworthy to deal fairly with them, don't think you can teach them anything. You can't. You may have them sitting down on the outside, but it's their insides you should be trying to win over. It can be done—I've proven it. It can be done through transparency, truth, and fairness (something adults have been far too short on for far too long). After all, at the end of every day, I require (not being perfect) just as much patience and love from Papa as they do. At the foot of the cross, even age doesn't matter. That's what I told them, too. Every so often, I would have someone I dealt with ask me what made me different from other LEOs. That's when I would take the opportunity to brag on my Papa. That I was simply extending to others what I needed and gratefully received from Him. I won't always be around, but Papa will, and I hope it stuck.

The more of Papa I got ahold of (the more of His love that permeated my soul), the less disdain (judgment) I found myself even wanting to have for others, no matter what situation they found themselves in.

One night, we were called to a hotel room to break up a fight. If you found yourself checking into this particular hotel, you were definitely on the downside of life. One of the suspects ran out and down the backside of the hotel right before we got there. An officer took off after him. The officer and the suspect were running blind. The direction he took off into was completely unlit and was a forgotten part of the landscape with a dilapidated road that lead off into a heavily wooded area. I had never been back there, neither had the officer who was giving chase. The pavement stopped abruptly at a deep ravine; it had collapsed years ago. Without any light and knowledge of the area, you were doomed to run right off into thin air, where gravity (enacting upon every object at 9.8 meters per second squared) would take you into an abyss, the bottom of which held unknown spike-like growths and shrapnel from at least a decade of doubling as the city dump.

It took all of us a while to find the officer who had given chase. We had lost radio contact with him. Losing radio contact with a fellow officer makes everyone a little nervous anyway, but losing contact with one whose previous traffic was obviously given under duress causes a surge of intensity that brings us all into a unified, laser-like focus. We tried cell phone contact as well. Having no luck on both fronts made finding our own brother far more important than anything else. While giving chase to the suspect, our brother had lost both his police radio and his cell phone. We finally found him after being reduced to the old-fashioned techniques of yelling and following the clues that get left behind in a recently disturbed area, which included his dropped police radio, and, within a few more feet, his cell phone. Eventually, he was found standing at the edge of the pavement overlooking the ravine.

The suspect had launched himself off into the dark and fell much farther than he anticipated. His landing, being far from eloquent, left his right leg from the knee down in a shattered state that could be seen from the distance under his attire of boots and jeans. The swelling and twisted shape made me cringe, and it was only growing larger. The suspect ran because we had five warrants for his arrest. They were not felony warrants; they were misdemeanor warrants. Meaning, he had just taken a *very serious* but meaningless risk that only by Papa's merciful hand he did not pay for with his life. If he had landed even a half foot in any other direction, he would have been impaled on the darkened spike-shaped foliage, or his head would have impacted an object that could have rendered him DOA. The one thing I had absolutely no desire to do was laugh. Understanding Papa's great love for you allows you to be *appropriate*. Meaning, that I was able to be as aggressive as necessary to contain any situation while being able to retain a considerable amount of mercy for each person as a human being also created in God's image. My brothers in blue did not share this commitment. They stood on the edge of the pavement, shining their flashlights down on him, laughing and making comments not only about the lack of intelligence the suspect had shown by getting himself into his present situation but also his lack of apparent concern for the whole of his life to end up with five warrants. My brother in blue and in Christ, John, was among them.

After a bit, I could no longer hold my peace. I quietly pulled John off to the side, as I had done other times with other officers, and very deliberately reminded him that we are all equal at the foot of the cross and that if not for the grace of God, that man at the bottom could have been me or him. John and I had that kind of relationship; he could remind me and I could remind him. He was always my favorite. Laughing at the downfall of others was a habit very easily fallen into in this line of work, and I had done my share of it as well. But the more in love I became with Papa, the less I could do it or even stomach listening to it. If this job taught me anything, it was most certainly that in some way, shape, or form, we were all going to have our turn on the "chopping block." Meaning, that due to the scrutiny our actions are *always* under, we were all going to be made fun of, thought ill of, or unfairly questioned/accused at any time.

Having God's grace define my work is what made my work not only worthwhile, but it also gave those I arrested the opportunity to admit they were wrong by always behaving as someone does when they "leave the door open" after correction is given. To have someone you've just arrested and taken to jail go from calling you every name in the book to shaking your hand and thanking you for dealing with them in love and respect was fantastic. This allows and literally draws out the treasure and good things in others for *change.* It gives hope. It is the *goodness of God* that leads men to repentance, not the mentality of "the beatings will continue until moral improves" or anything close to "I told you so." Anyone can be a "bully with a badge." Still, no matter how nice you may wish to be, there will always be those who respond to nothing else except force (a different form of love). In these cases, "HOPE" gets served up on a completely different platter. In those rare cases, I cannot help but say, "Okay, if that's the way you want it, let the fun begin."

Usually, it's a case of "hurting people who are hurting people." And sometimes it's a case of the terribly passive and permissive parent who is now incapable of defending him or herself against the monster they created who is now an adult. These monsters have an entitlement mind-set that is so severe the only thing that will move them is force. It's sad really. All the characters the offender should have been required to obtain as a child is now being demanded from them as an adult. Sadly, their vast incapability is now requiring us to unleash an adult-sized whoopin' on him or her in a simple effort to keep anyone from being hurt—including the offender.

This puts me in mind of someone we'll call "Melanie." She was a thirty-two-year-old, almost-six-feet, three-hundred-plus-pound female hold up in the basement of her eighty-plus-year-old grandmother's house. The grandmother had had enough. Melanie was horrible. We showed up, tiptoed through the wake of broken glass (she had thrown quite a fit), and waded into the bowels of the grandmother's home. Melanie was tucked away in the rows of boxes and intently screaming, "Get out of my house! Leave me alone!"

Shortly after each scream, the owner of the home said, "Get her out of here." Well, we were in for a fight, my friends. Please, not the fight for our lives or anything close; however, she did become "my baby" because she was...well...a SHE! Unfortunately, the shortest path between the nearest exit and my patrol car was the driveway she had littered with Grandma's pretties that were now just an obstacle course of broken glass. So guess what? That's right. This biatch got dragged over the glass SHE broke. (She REFUSED TO WALK.) She was dragged by every limb she had available after all other attempts to peacefully remove her had failed.

The game changer was when she launched herself out from the boxes toward me and knocked me up against a wall. The officer in charge of the call yelled, "NO ONE HITS ONE OF MY OFFICERS!" And it got real...for her anyway. Once she got forced into my car, she whimpered and cried. Then, once she got to the jail, she absolutely refused to get out of the car. I talked, I reasoned...no freakin' way. So, another officer got the feet while I got the head and quite eloquently reminded her that this was GOING TO HAPPEN! It wasn't graceful, but it worked out. Once inside, the all-male staff pleadingly requested that I do the strip search. What can I say? This job is NOT all glitz and glamour! She refused to cooperate, too.

No one got physically injured (seriously Amazing Grace over that one), not even Melanie.

I remember each and every time either one of my boys, in their first attempts at complete control (usually you see this around three years old), stomped their little foot at me, their bodies squared off with their eyes locked on mine as they yelled "NO!" to a request I had given them. I saw these spoiled adult monsters in the same light. They were coddled as children and had always been comforted by someone that nothing was ever their responsibility or fault. Someone was always cleaning up their mess while they looked on in control. As far as I was concerned, my goal was the same with them as it had been with my boys: bring them back to reality so they *can learn*. No one can learn as long as they're busy being completely focused on doing their own thing or having their own way. It just doesn't work. A spanking is a *tool* like any other to bring someone to the place where they can listen and truly hear, so they can learn and change. Discipline by spanking is *not wrong*, and it cannot possibly be abused when it is used with that mind-set. That mind-set does not even allow for anger. Time-outs or other popular replacements, like any disciplinary action, can be and is abused. The abuse is the belittling attitude the authority figure takes, which states or implies the child is dumb, stupid, or worthless. That, as we all know, can be easily done without even touching a child. I was very proud of our PD when it came to spankings. We knew the difference between child abuse and spankings. Having chunks of skin removed from repeated lashings with a tree branch is NOT a spanking. We would have juveniles come to the PD to report the adults in their lives for child abuse all because they didn't want to be spanked. Sorry, not gonna work.

The Taser that LEOs carry is what I called "the adult spanking." I loved that little guy. Thousands of volts of absolutely harmless electricity (it's the amps that kill) would cause the most vicious of characters to promise they'd never misbehave again. It came in handy. Not laughing at the downfall of others did not (nor could it) keep me from a hearty chuckle upon hearing a six-foot-plus, tattooed badass of a man whimper, "Please, please don't Tase me, Bro! I've been shot. I've been stabbed, and I never...please, I'll be good I promise!" This came shortly after his deliberate threat to kill any one of us who tried to arrest him. The Taser was also very good at turning the incoherent ramblings of a backstreet thug into the amazing grammatical excellence of a college graduate. On a DV (domestic violence) call, I rushed into a home to back up my brother who was dealing with a man who insisted on escalating the situation even though my partner was doing an awesome job keeping his cool. The offender's girlfriend was sitting outside with bruises on her face and neck. The finger marks were so apparent you could easily match his grip with her bruising. As it became more apparent to the offender that he was going to get arrested, his "thug lingo" got thicker and thicker as his behavior and arm waving became more agitated. I walked in (I don't look like much); the offender took one look at me. And, as was par for the course, he totally dismissed my presence. I'm okay with that. Underestimation from others was a fantastic opportunity I utilized to my advantage frequently. My partner's back was to me. I quietly unsnapped my Taser from its holster and held it out for the offender to see—seriously...I just showed it to him. I didn't turn it on or anything. He stopped in mid-sentence and became exquisitely articulate in admitting his guilt, and that he was ready to cooperate. The offender held both his wrists together for ease in handcuffing. I wasn't looking for all that! I just wanted to suggest that he tame it down. That mental image still makes me chuckle. All I ever wanted was change. The question always was: what was it going to take? The answer was completely up to the individual(s) on scene.

The Taser, with all its voltage, proved to be barely a match for the increasing use of prescription drugs mixed with alcohol. It only takes a few encounters with Klonopin to know this. One dose of Klonopin mixed with only one or two beers make the consumer behave as though they've had enough alcohol to render them completely inept at everything—even conversation. A young woman in her early twenties required five Taser deployments to *safely* affect her arrest—yes, I said "safely" and not in regards to me. (Quite frankly, I. WILL. WIN. *They* were the only person I was ever worried about.) When someone went "crazy" on me during an arrest, my goal was to try to complete the arrest with as little injury to the offender as possible. I know the general public likes to whine and moan over Taser usage, but let me ask you this: if you're gonna get stupid, would you rather wake up with injuries that could include legally broken limbs or joints, or wake up with a bump on your gut or thigh from a Taser hit? That Taser *will get* compliance (I believe that is what the public is really whining and moaning about—they hate the fact we can actually *make* them obey), and so will a legal nightstick strike to the leg, limbs, or torso. But during a struggle, when the offender is not going to guarantee your strike is not to their joints or easily broken limbs, I far preferred the instant compliance I received when deploying my Taser even for one second. The problem in this instance, with this young woman, was that she had taken Klonopin and consumed alcohol. That combo gives the offender the memory capacity you could shove up a gnat's ass and have room left over. You had about a ten-second window before whatever your encounter achieved was completely forgotten, and you started over as if you had just met them. That's why it took five deployments. Each deployment lasted no more than a second, but I would always stop *because I gained full compliance.* In a matter of ten seconds—here we would go again. Even in handcuffs she bit, fought, and kicked, and even put her feet on either side of the doorframe to keep me from placing her in my vehicle. Another deployment got her in the car very gracefully. Then WHAM! Off she went again, kicking my windows and screaming. I'll never forget her and not for the reasons you think.

Several months later, I was in the courtroom to testify to the cases I had made on that docket. I saw this expertly dressed young woman eyeballing me pretty hard. She wasn't "mean mugging" me; her eyes were just fixed, and I knew I should probably recognize her—but I didn't. Her entire appearance was suggestive of a life well put together.

Finally, she left her seat and came walking up to me and asked if I remembered her. She introduced herself and quickly jogged my memory of how we met. It was that same young woman I had arrested. She had woken up the next day with no memory of what had happened. She said she read my arrest report and saw video footage of her behavior, and she found herself embarrassed and appalled. She then threw her arms around me and thanked me for not only what she saw I did but also for what I *didn't* do. She thanked me for the fact that she woke up with bee-stung-sized bumps on her leg and not a broken limb or any of the other numerous things that will most likely happen when you are engaged in a physical altercation. She said she had a child at home and did not need to be acting that way, and I had found her at the bottom of a "downhill slide" from which she had received her wake-up call. *That's what I'm talking about! Change!* Papa's obvious interest in the lives of others never ceases to amaze me. He led me during that encounter every step of the way.

Chapter Six

A question I get a lot is this: how do you get a shift of high-octane leaders to work together on a call? It's pretty simple really. The officer who arrives on the scene first is the lead; the rest are backup/support. This means you won't always agree with how things go down. In the beginning, when I first started working with my shift, I usually found myself disagreeing with the initial assessment *and* the decisions that were made when it came to DV calls. These guys just didn't get it. Only time would tell whether they just didn't *know* or didn't *want to know* (didn't care). What I liked about my shift was that we had a wide variety of ages. I think the youngest officer we had was twenty-seven, with the oldest being fifty-two. Papa helped me and gave me wisdom with them, too. I wanted acceptance from them, like anyone else—but I wanted to sleep with a clear conscience, too, and sometimes the two didn't always match up. They would simply have to learn—and they did. One of the things I am very proud of is—because of the wisdom Papa clearly demonstrated through me with DV calls—I began to gain a silent reputation on my shift. This group of high-octane personalities who inherently cared more for fights than for understanding others began to ask me questions privately after they began to allow me to help them handle emotionally packed affairs which required more than barking out orders if we truly wished not to return in an hour or so. They began to ask me why people did what they did. Why do they stay and why don't the victims "see"? I enjoyed the fact that even the most brutish officer, although he struggled with my answers, wanted to know what drove these people's choices. I watched with silent appreciation as I began to see these officers take what I said and become better at dealing with people. It still brings a smile to my face. They also called me the "dog whisperer" (Ha!), but more on that later when I make an attempt to show you the lighter side of all this.

Is it a compliment at all to say that I had a way with folks other officers labeled as "crazy"? I think so. I have a soft spot for rejected people, I admit it (I am one, so was Christ); but so does Papa, and I'm proud to be just like Him. Concerning DV, no matter how much education you offer, not knowing when and how to ask *the right* questions was going to draw you to a bad conclusion and keep you on the scene far longer than you need to be. Over the course of my service, DV cases doubled every year. With a bad economy, it is true that you will always see a rise in DV and DUI cases. With my background and Papa's wisdom, I proved to be a very unique professional, like a regular "Sherlock Holmes" when it came to domestic violence. This brings me to a call out in the county. This story is proof that no matter how careful, transparent, or fair you try to be, and no matter how you bring an end to someone else's bad evening, it was going to be a completely "effed" up situation.

Calls out in the county were usually pretty "noteworthy." The folks out in the county tended to be a tad bit more serious about the trouble they caused. They had usually moved that far out so they could do what they wanted. Not having to follow city-limit rules while being farther away gave them more time to get trouble going and keep it going.

I was the last of three officers to arrive. Houses, addresses, and driveways were sometimes virtually impossible to find. Since two others had already arrived, I was about to cancel myself from the call to prevent "pile up." It was a busy night, after all. But then the leading officer requested I show up. I figured he wanted me because I could pat down a female much more completely than they could, and, by now, the guys respected my knowledge of the dysfunctional "crazies" as they called them. I finally found the driveway and parked at the base. I had no idea this call was going to challenge everything I knew for the next eight very long hours.

As I walked up this crevice-infested drive, there was a hefty early-twenties female covered in her own blood, sitting about halfway up. We will call her Sarah. A neatly dressed man and woman who appeared to be in their fifties, along with a younger teenage female, stood solemnly (and unnaturally composed) in a group at the top with the lead officer. Unless Sarah ran her own face into the bricks on that house, I figured the dad was going to jail. At first glance, this was my guess: Sarah was the estranged daughter of the man who stood with his common-law wife (he had under control), and the teenage girl was their child in common who was the "favored" offspring. Sarah's attire and present sobbing state reeked of an abused daughter who had a string of very bad choices, one of which included being here at this address. The solemn stares and gestures from the older man at the top towards Sarah suggested complete rejection of her very existence. I've seen that look before, from my own rented parent. The time of night combined with circumstances told me that Sarah wasn't there to win her daddy's approval (that ship had sailed) but was there as the end result of believing a lie and being lured. She reeked of frustrated powerlessness. I know that look, too. Daddy loomed from above with power.

Now, before you accuse me of not being objective because of my past, let me point out to all parents who actually DO love their children some very important facts. In any volatile situation, it is fairly easy to tell, with some practice, which parts have been "staged or planned" and which parts are straight from the hip (aka, the truth). When could you *ever* stand *at a distance* and LORD OVER your own child covered in their own blood, even if they were wrong? A *loving* mother or father can't. If they can, then they'd be crazy and proving it by acting a fool by now. If the mother couldn't run to her child because of the control of the male present, she would show signs of severe agitation, and the male would be demonstrating signs of trying to keep the mother under control. None of those things were present. So that meant the older woman was more than likely *not* the biological mother. However, an abusive and twisted father can and *will* stand there and watch his own child die if it suited his purposes. I've lived it myself and have watched them do it. It was obvious to me that the teenager was favored and also knew better than to speak a word. Her physical position showed unison while her body language and tense face (eyes glancing toward her daddy) suggested forced or at the very least uncomfortable compliance. I was support, not lead, and to be honest, sometimes the one with the most legal recourse holds the cards (that was daddy on this one because it was his property). No matter how this turned out, the most I was capable of was "damage control." Damage control was what I called my best effort to gain the cooperation of and help the victims I felt had gotten shortchanged by the lead officer's decisions.

I was called to try and see if I could get Sarah to cooperate. She would not let anyone near her. She was, as they love to say, "crazy"; I called it hysterical. The call was dispatched as a DV, and, supposedly, a "crazy woman was ramming the caller's house with her Jeep." Keep in mind, the dispatcher can only relay the info they get (true or not) from the caller. In this case, the father was the caller. At first glance, common sense told me that Sarah, being the only one bleeding with a busted face and head, was the victim. But because there were a few scratches on her vehicle to support the father's claim she was trying to ram the house, it also made her look like the primary aggressor (along with having to drive to the other side of town to do it). There was no damage to the house, not even a spot. There was *nothing*, I felt, to back up dad's claim that the tree branch he used to "defend" himself on her face and head was necessary. Nothing, of course, except the controlled common-law wife and teenage daughter. Sarah had been lured there by the sweet promises of her estranged family that they would care for her infant son while she had a night out with friends. (I'm sure I'm starting to sound less impartial.) Upon her return, they had refused to return the child to her. This setup was the fuse, fuel, and catalyst for stupid. I did mention that I did not always agree with the lead officer, didn't I? The lead officer tasked me with arresting—wait for it—Sarah. I did make my objections, having Sarah's side of the story that answered for every wound on her body and even where the offending tree branch had been cast. My money was on her for honesty. Her entire demeanor of nothing to lose combined with a story she *did not* have to carefully consider as she told it made it fairly easy to understand what happened. Sometimes the lead officer would demonstrate behavior that I came to realize meant, "I don't have a clue. I'm in over my head on this one, and I have to make a decision *now*." I was begging Papa for help on this one. Even by state law, I felt there should have at least been a dual arrest made, but it wasn't my call. How in the world was I going to get Sarah to cooperate and trust me when I was the one to betray her by an arrest? My grasp on her trust was tenuous at best. For an adult child of abuse to trust anyone was, as my dedication page stated, an act of valor, and Sarah wasn't feeling it. I had to follow orders, and before you give up on me, Papa showed me that it would actually be best for Sarah *and safer* if she left with me—even to jail.

This girl was a mess and not a hot mess either. In her twenties and clueless as ever, she was caught on a man's property that held all the legal cards. She had been tricked into coming out there, and all they had to do was get her started and let stupidity take it from there. The only way she was getting off that land safely and staying off was in my car. Crazy people had a tendency to get crazier when their fears of "trusting in the system" come true. They're not lawyers, know nothing of law, and feel completely powerless (they still think it's all about "fair," which is far more subjective than most people realize). Not always, but I could usually calm somebody down by educating them on the cards they *did* hold. Sarah proved to be one hell of a student.

I convinced her that I was trying to keep her safe, and that if she would continue to trust me, I could help her. She was a complicated mix of needing convincing and needing an authority. Pulling the wrong one at the wrong time caused her to fly into hysterics. The worst outcome you can have in dealing with an abused terrified person is brought on by physically handling them, but the worst outcome you can have with an immature stubborn person is brought on by verbally handling them. She was both.

Think for a moment. How hard is it for you to get someone who really knows you to trust you minute by minute when what you're trying to lead them to is a surprise party or something else good? Now, how hard do you think it is to get a total stranger to trust you minute to minute, with nothing to guide them, that you're even worth it? See my point? I couldn't take her to the car and give her the play by play and explain, "Well, this is the plan...see how it's going to work out for you?" I didn't have the play by play. Papa was giving it to me right when I needed it. This was step by step.

I knew the jail would not take her, but I couldn't tell her that. As I put the handcuffs on, I was explaining that this is necessary, and I would remove them ASAP. She fought the episodes of hysteria with simple pleas to affirm whether or not I was trustworthy. Once we pulled up outside the jail, she went nuts. She claimed I had tricked her. I gave her a stern look, and with calm assurance, I said, "We're not done yet, are we?" She fell to a protested silence. Seeing as how I had trouble trusting Papa minute by minute, I have to say I admired her trust in me. I took her inside and had a chat with the jailer I knew well. I quickly gave her the overview, including the fact that I'm following protocol to bring her here, and asked if she could do me the favor of calling my lieutenant and put her foot down on accepting Sarah. Sarah, legally, was mine until someone else officially took her from me—damage control—that wasn't going to happen. I can play the system, too; I just very rarely did so. Quite honestly, this was the first time Papa lead me through the maze of playing the system's loopholes for the benefit of another. It warms my heart to know that Papa cared enough for her to do so.

Sarah's face was swollen. The bridge of her nose was black and blue, and the egg-shaped lump on the back of her head was still open. It was easy for the jailer to reject her until she had the proper medical attention. Oh, my lieutenant was going to hate me for this (smile). This meant he *had* to give me permission to take her to the ER, and I *had* to stay with her until x-rays, assessments, and medications were all taken care of. Have you ever been to an ER? Exactly. See, this was going to work out for Sarah. I told Sarah she would not be going to jail, so her reaction to my pulling up to it was natural, but certain things had to play out undisturbed. With a Papa-style nudge, things would roll in the right direction. Anytime someone is jailed for DV, there is a twelve-hour cooling off period (from the time of arrest, NOT incarceration), where no bail can be made. By the time I was done with her, those twelve hours were going be all but gone. I was going to drop her off at the metro with nothing left to do but sign her own bond. Also, I knew that from the center of town (the jail), she had someone to call who would come get her. From out in the county, she was SOL. Thanks, Papa, this plan was perfect.

A theory I've had for decades was proven very accurate (at least with Sarah) during my eight hours with her. She had been diagnosed with a list of mental illnesses. I had to survive the tumultuous rabbit holes of thought processes that made up this woman. Well, I didn't *have* to, but I was curious.

Every time she started spouting seemingly unrelated non-sense, I began to ask questions instead of ignoring her. The answers she gave affirmed the belief I've had that if you abuse someone long enough and combine it with the right personality and circumstances, the result is a very legitimate and bizarre mind filled with twisted tunnels of reasoning that produce almost delusional conclusions about life, about others, and about what their role on the earth is. *Voila!* Mental illness (some, anyway). I used to be anti-medication back in my cultishly religious days. Sarah would need drugs. I needed drugs. However, my intensions were, what I can only assume, different than most. I would use the drugs only as long as I had to, helping me while I unwind all the serpentine thinking placed there by my undeserving parent. Some people have been so twisted like a beaten dog; they're now programmed to do only one thing—self-destruct. For those like me, like Sarah, there is no way out of this "matrixly" twisted construct without an Almighty God; I don't care how many or what kind of drugs you have. Papa is the only one who can deliver you out of such a deep-rooted mess. It is satanic.

Her logic was undeniable and made complete sense to me on any given topic or paranoia. I asked Papa for the ability to go with her and follow her twisted mind, but not to lose my way. Each topic of conversation was a puzzle of deep, dark, twisted, and logical paths which produced the effortless conclusions that were completely wrong but also completely undeniable. Survival tactics don't work once you're all grown up, and she had no idea how to change gears.

Imagine throwing God or religion into all this mess! That's where you get the parents who do what Sarah's dad did and can quote scripture out of the 1611 King James Version to back it up. Been there, done that, too. That's where the "Black and White" poem comes from and my anger against manipulative pastors (probably with abusive pasts of their own) who beat their congregation with fear and preach a list of exterior behaviors as proof of righteousness. Putting God into an already twisted mix gives you this next story.

One night, before I was cut loose (passed initial training to perform the duties of an LEO on my own), my handler (as I called him) and I found a woman parked in front of the Salvation Army store. She was completely distraught, and it looked like everything she owned was in the back of her car. It was about 0300 – 0400, and my handler, still wanting to show me how it's done, made first contact. She had, while everyone slept at her house, packed her car quickly in an attempt to flee from the mind control she felt she was under. My handler glanced at me with an expression that said, "Here's another crazy one." Don't get mad at these guys—it's not that they don't care...*they don't know*. I like to think of it this way: if you don't know what I'm talking about, then Praise God! It means you haven't been through it. Finding those who understand me is both a blessing and a hurt. If they get me or I get them, it's only because they've been hurt, too, in the same ways. I want to be understood but hate knowing someone else has been hurt as deeply to do so.

It's been several years since my encounter with this woman, and it's very difficult to get people to start at an intelligible beginning. When you find them, so much has happened...where, oh, where to begin. She babbled on in what seemed like jumbled pieces that did not fit together. We could understand the words she was speaking but they just didn't make any sense together. Then she used a term I was familiar with: eisegesis (look it up). My spirit began to jump up and down. "You know what she's been through!" In that split second, every seemingly unconnected piece of jumbled verbiage she had uttered turned into a masterpiece to me. I very enthusiastically took the lead from my handler and said, "You're trying to escape from a cult, aren't you?" As my handler looked at me with a very obvious case of *"How the hell did you draw that conclusion!"* this woman, who was barely keeping it together, completely lost it and began sobbing and snotting all over herself. Right before she surrendered herself to total sob mode, she looked at me and mouthed the words, "Oh, my God! You know!" She sobbed so badly my handler got a little concerned and tried to get her to affirm she did not need medical attention. After that, since the night was slow, my handler, in demeanor, backed off and decided to simply be a spectator. I think he knew he was in over his head on this one.

I knew exactly how she felt, and I knew exactly what was going on. Details can be whatever they want—the basics remain the same—control is control. However long she had been where she had—under someone's control with her family in the mix—the sobbing she was doing now was the release from getting probably the only affirmation she had ever received that she was not the crazy one; those in her cult were. With renewed awe, I stop and think that Papa knows just exactly who we need to come in contact with.

She had been under a pastor and husband who were manipulative and controlling. Manipulative control by hanging the threat of rejection from God is *not* taken lightly by someone who sincerely fears being wrong with Papa and fears rejection overall. Those of us who come from abusive backgrounds are way too easily held fast through fear on this type of theology that someone else can prove (using scripture, of course). I have learned this the hard way: *do not* believe everything someone else can prove. I gave her the shortened version of my own flight from religious control. She already believed I could help; my testimony was icing on the cake. I gave her the same advise I was given back then—RUN! Of course, now, I was able to inform her of the outcome—I never looked back, and I have never been better. God absolutely loves you (I added), and He's not mad at you!

The most convincing of cults or denominations that have cultish, fear-based tactics all seem to use the King James 1611 Bible. "If it ain't KJV—it ain't Bible." I can still hear that being blasted from the pulpit of the Independent Fundamental

Baptist Church I used to go to. A mighty fist pounding to the solid wooden pulpit always followed it. It's not the Bible version that's important (although I do think it's odd that all the ministries that keep their people under strict control kind of all agree about that one), it's the way they spout hatred and absolute intolerance of others and use scripture to back it all up. They also encourage isolation among the members to keep from being polluted. As my poem, "Black and White" states, you cannot shoot people (judge them) and love them, too; it is not, nor has it ever been, possible.

My entire family, at one time, was held fast by a hate mongering, fear-based IFB Church (Independent Fundamental Baptist). Their tactics were every bit cultish, and NO, they're not the only denomination that does this. I have found all levels of this tactic in *every* denomination. There was no compound built or bars on the windows, but ask anyone of its members if they could leave and join another church. Whatever their answer, it was going to pale in comparison to the fearful look on their face and the undeniable agitation in their voice. As easy to leave as it may sound for some, it will take everything you have for others. I sincerely hope that woman found her strength and courage and took Papa's nudge to leave to heart. Once she collected herself, we had a delightful conversation that my handler simply put up with but could not follow. That was okay. I had tissues, and by the time it was over, she had her feet back under her.

For some of us, there's a splinter in the back of our minds that just won't go away. It keeps pulling at the hope within us that just can't let go of the idea that we're not free; that everyone else has it wrong somehow, and we haven't truly found God's love. *Listen to it!*

Chapter Seven

The number 7 in the Scriptures has always been taught to me as the number of completion. Although I had not planned this to be the final chapter, it is fitting, wouldn't you say? As I was contemplating with Papa whether or not this work was truly done, He expressed His desire that this book be finished with an adamant recap of just how wonderfully loved I am. How loved I am is exactly how loved *you are*. You are His favorite.

In this world of hatefully screwed up parents who abuse, play favorites, belittle, abandon, manipulate, control, beat down, and justify it all, I wish to remind you of what Papa had me say earlier:

He does the work and I feel the pain.
He wipes my tears and says, "Please, try again.
This battle's not over it's only begun.
Trust ME my child and please do not run.
To see it all now, there'll be no room for Faith.
You WILL see my Glory you WILL have a taste.
I know that all you are able to see
Is the loss you think was created by Me.
I was not the one that created

Your life of pain that inundated
You with failure, fear and doubt;
Watch ME now as I clean it all out!
I'll put your feet on solid ground,
You'll be stronger, I promise and my promise is sound.
I will do what you let ME now please, be still!
I was with you through pain; I honored free will.
Now you—look at ME and keep your eyes fast
I will uphold your future and bury your past.
This pain will never touch you again.
My Grace will abound and MY WILL, WILL WIN.
These people that used you and left you behind—
I did NOT send them they were NOT Mine!
But if you will let Me, the power of GRACE
Will heal each scar, each pain and each face
And replace them with those that will keep you as dear
As I do. Now rest in My hands, right here."

He has done for me just as He promised. That section of
poetry was written in hope several years ago. I am here to tell
you, He has accomplished it. I can stay as mad at Papa as I
chose to, believing that if He loved me so much why in the
world did He even let any of my past happen? If you stop and
consider the scope of control you are actually asking Him to
impose on another human being, you will quickly find that
He will have to eventually impose control upon you—even
when you think you're right, so as not to allow you to infringe
upon another's life in a negative fashion. We could all be a
puppet, that's not what He's after. Truth is we demand free
will when it's about us wanting to do or go but we want His
intervention when we scream "unfair." I took the hard road
to being whole. *You don't have to.* I tried to impose religious
strategies on myself that I believed to be pleasing to God, only
to find out I had simply warped His teachings to fit within my
already *very* warped understanding of love: do good, get acceptance (maybe); do bad, get rejected (definitely). I believe

those pastors meant well. But I can't help but also believe that they too grew up with a warped definition of love. I believe one of the reasons He had me write this is to try to prevent others from doing the same or catch those in the middle and help them escape. He loves you so much. I know this because He is, figuratively speaking, a "bee in my bonnet," until I got this book done and submitted for publishing! He really wants you to have this!

He supernaturally intervened in my life as a child and literally wiped my mind clean of the years of gruesome detail I could have had concerning the sexual abuse I lived through. He does that so often to so many children. As a matter of fact, it is a well-documented occurrence in psychiatric studies. He left only as many clues as I needed to have so that in His timing, when I came across someone He had specially trained to recognize those clues, he could do so, so that I could move forward. The road He set me on to set me free from my past also set me free from ALL the forms of bondage my past helped create with the biggie being self-condemnation. Listen carefully: *God is not the author of guilt; God is not the author of conditional acceptance of the believer.* His acceptance into heaven is only conditional to those who have not taken Him up on His offer of forgiveness and accepted His one and only Son as payment for their sins (John 3:16).

I was told, on more than one occasion, that I would be in counselor's offices and on meds for the rest of my life simply in the *effort* to achieve some life that could be considered "normal." The greatest testimony I feel I have is that I don't care who you are. After meeting me and getting to know me, you would *never* suspect even a hint of the background that is actually mine! Truly, in the world of psychology, I am a medical miracle. I am as much a medical miracle as someone who wins a sports medal after having been paralyzed from the neck down and told there is nothing that can be done. It's true. Now, you can't make me believe He doesn't love me. I am as certain of His love for me now as I used to be of His disdain for my very existence. One day, if you, too, are in doubt, you will never again believe He doesn't love you (well, not with any validity anyway). I love what Papa told me one day as I contemplated the memory I have of believing I was His "whipping boy." He said, "I had a whipping boy. His name is *Jesus!*" For those of you who may not understand the antiquated term "whipping boy," it was the person the master of the house had chosen to beat or otherwise discipline, because he was angry and needed someone to take it out on.

I couldn't see or articulate any of this until just this year (2012), not entirely, anyway. I had to battle some straggling ailments that finally released their hold as I begin to really get ahold of His love for me; the depth, the height, and the width of it will be something I will get to explore for all of eternity starting yesterday (Ha!). It really is that inexhaustible.

My life is not normal; it is *better than normal!* I know a lot of normal people who do not contain even half the joy I know every day. I know a lot of defeated normal people. Their hope is they will maintain enough health to get to their retirement years so that the retirement they hoped will be there will hopefully be enough to keep them from having to supplement. I don't hope…I know. I have not only gotten to normal, but I have passed it to *abundance*. I'm fully aware of who I am, that I shouldn't be alive much less a successful contributor to the lives, hopes, and dreams of others. If someone with my past survives, they are, at best, a drain on society. Not by choice, however; they simply don't know they are loved. So here I am: a walking, living, breathing, completed testimony of His abundant love. My only endeavor for the rest of my years is to ensure, as much as God will supply me the opportunity, that after we meet, you will walk a little taller, be a little brighter, and land a little farther ahead on your own road to completion by the Hope that speaks to your soul as it did to mine: "You know He will win."